A Heart for Imbabura

A Heart for Imbabura

The Story of Evelyn Rychner

Charles W. Shepson

Christian Publications

CAMP HILL, PENNSYLVANIA

Christian Publications
3825 Hartzdale Drive, Camp Hill, PA 17011

The mark of ✝ *vibrant faith*

ISBN: 0-87509-482-1
LOC Catalog Card Number: 91-77847
© 1992 by Christian Publications

92 93 94 95 96   5 4 3 2 1

Cover illustration
© 1992, Karl Foster

Publisher's Statement

Every effort has been made to present the facts of this story as accurately as possible and to remain true to the history of the persecution, growth and development of the evangelical church in Ecuador. The facts can be substantiated both in Ecuador and in North American literature. There is no intent to malign or wound any denomination, especially in light of the favorable shift in attitude towards evangelicals in Latin America in the last 20 to 30 years.

DEDICATION

This book is dedicated to

THE LIVING LORD *of*

the twelve, *who prayed daily for me during the
writing of these chapters.*

the five, *who read every word of this manuscript to
make suggestions and corrections.*

the uncomplaining book widow, *my sweetheart, who
was also among the twelve and the five.*

the subject of this book, *whose impeccable reputation
commands my highest respect.*

the rainbow, *Who decided that the time had come to
rescue it from the enemy who had stolen
it away.*

the universe, *including Imbabura Province.*

Contents

Preface

This book is the story of Evelyn Rychner, missionary to Ecuador, South America.

The marvelous things accomplished in and through her life are a credit to her Lord who chose to work through her exceptional level of commitment rather than through any special talents or giftedness she may have possessed.

Persistence, optimism, love for the unlovely and unconditional willingness to serve are earthtones not nearly as colorful as personal charisma or super intelligence or outstanding giftedness. Yet for some reason, known only to Himself, God chooses the former palette for His paintbrush much more frequently than the latter.

So don't look for a string of miracles. That's not why Evelyn Rychner was chosen as a subject for the Jaffray Series. Simply prepare your heart to experience the thrill of elusive and hard-won victory, extra sweet because it blossoms slowly, laboriously unfolded, nourished by the acid soil of opposition, adversity, hardship and shattered hopes and dreams.

The faithfulness of a faithful God to His faithful servant produces both the beauty and the fragrance of the blossom that opens in its glory at the end of this book.

1

Unusual Siamese Twins

God first placed a burden for the Indians in the Province of Imbabura (pronounced Eem-bah-boo´-rah) upon the heart of Homer Gail Crisman. He was one of the first missionaries to enter Ecuador in 1911 when the doors were thrown open by the adoption of a new constitution that guaranteed religious liberty. This constitution and the liberty it espoused would become, as we shall see, a critical factor in the evangelization of Imbabura.

Crisman had heard that there was a large tribe of Indians—over 100,000—living in the high Andes up near the Colombian border. They had no gospel witness and there was no road to take him to them. The high mountains and deep ravines between civilization and the inhabitants of Imbabura would necessitate a grueling, two-day horseback ride.

Crisman headed out. Bouncing along hour after hour, he prayed: "Lord, lead me to the right man who will lead me to the right spot where we can establish a church in Imbabura."

This prayer would be answered sooner than Crisman could have dreamed.

Night was closing in fast. It always does at the equator. Crisman booked into a tambo (inn). That night also, an Indian, enroute to his thatched-roof, mud-walled home near the town of Otavalo, was registered at the inn. Crisman deposited his meager baggage in the crude accommodation. Pulling the door shut behind him, he headed out in search of the "right man." The cool, mountain air felt invigorating.

The Indian from Otavalo was leaning against the mud wall of the tambo. Long, braided, shiny, black hair trailed down his bright red poncho from beneath a felt hat. His calloused feet were bare.

"Buenas tardes," Crisman began as he squatted beside the Indian. "I'm looking for a place in the center of Indian territory where we can establish a Mission station—a place where we can tell people about God, where we can hold reading and writing classes, where we can work together toward a richer life on this earth."

The Quichua* (pronounced Key´-choo-ah) Indian studied the white man's face. Finally, after what seemed more like minutes than seconds, he replied, "I know just the place for you!" His enthusiasm was uncharacteristic. "Agato (Ah-gah´-toh). There is a piece of land

*Quichua is the correct spelling in Ecuador.

you can buy in Agato."

Even Mr. Crisman didn't realize what a miracle was being performed at that moment. The Indians were not normally of a mind to relinquish their land to white men, and most certainly not to the hated evangelicals.

The next day, the two men headed over the rugged mountains and around the shores of Lake San Pablo. The trail led up the slopes of Taita (Father) Imbabura, a towering, snow-capped peak. Finally at Agato, the Indian stopped abruptly and pointed to a rocky knoll. Crisman climbed to the crest of the knoll.

What a spectacle greeted him! In every direction, as far as the eye could see, Indian huts, surrounded by patches of farmland, dotted the landscape.

"This is just the place I am looking for," Crisman said to the Indian. Then he breathed skyward, "Surely You have led me here!"

The land, knoll included, was immediately available. This was God's provision. Crisman purchased it. Yes, Agato would be the place where the missionaries of The Christian and Missionary Alliance would challenge the reign of Satan in Imbabura. And what's more, they would emerge victorious. The spiritual seed that would be planted and scattered from this rocky knoll would be unlike any that had ever before germinated on the slopes of Father Imbabura, as the Indians reverently called that magnificent mountain.

It was not until the year following the initial purchase that the Mission decided to send the first missionary couple to Agato. Howard Cragin, his wife, Clara, and one-and-a-half-year-old Rebecca became the talk of the area. What a stir their arrival created! Norte (Nor´-teh) Americanos were as rare a sight in this part of the country as the giant condor birds. Dark, piercing eyes stared out from every doorway as the Cragins walked the trails that crisscrossed both the mountain towns and the countryside surrounding.

One day the Cragins stopped to refresh themselves by Lake San Pablo. Indian women were pounding out their wash on rocks by the stream that flowed from the large blue lake. One of those ladies, Rosa, chatted shyly but amiably with Clara Cragin.

To Rosa, it was almost inconceivable that this gringo family intended to live among them in one of their huts up in Agato. Others, like Rosa, were also intrigued by the prospect. Still others were infuriated at the thought of white people building on "their" property.

Rosa finished washing her clothes. Hurriedly tying her little niñita on her back, she adjusted the load so that both she and the baby would be comfortable. Rosa guided the Cragins further up the slopes of Taita Imbabura to Pedro Arias, the owner of a house that had recently been vacated. That windowless hut with the thatched roof became the home of the Cragins while they built a two-storied, adobe Mission house. Though constructed of hard-packed mud and with walls three feet thick, the Mission house was nevertheless somewhat crude by today's standards. But in the eyes of the Indians it was a mansion. There was no other building quite like it in Agato. Only in Otavalo, a few miles down the trail, were there houses that could even compare with it.

Bitter opposition flared as news of the Cragins' arrival spread through the area. The foundation and the walls of the house continued to rise. The construction laborers on their way to work each day carried axes to discourage attacks by bands of Indians angry at the laborers' apparent support of the Cragins. Religious leaders, too, stirred up hatred against the "white heretics." Other locals resented the ignominy of losing a piece of their precious land to gringos.

While the house was being constructed, the Cragins established a small clinic where the many maladies of the Indians could be treated. In the annual report of 1918 Howard Cragin wrote: "At the same time of the construction, we were careful to use every opportunity to give testimony of our Christian love, establishing a little clinic for curations of wounds, burns, extraction of teeth and to give simple remedies for curing the common ills. We always accompanied each curation with prayer in Spanish or Quichua."

The Cragins' loving help was welcomed by the Indians, at least by those with sufficient courage to put aside their fears of these "devils." Despite strong warnings against the missionaries, the Indians kept coming to the clinic. Desperation, it seemed, had a way of overcoming prejudice.

Unable to stop the incursion of these evangelicals, the religious leaders down in Otavalo incited an uprising.

"You must get rid of the Cragins," the priest told his followers, "peaceably, if possible; and if not, by means of clubs and stones."

One morning, by 10 a.m., a crowd of 150 Indians and whites (Spanish origin) began their march toward Agato, eager to carry out the priest's orders to "get rid of the Cragins."

"Down with the heretics!" the advancing mob shouted angrily. "We want to kill them all!"

As the procession arrived at the Mission house, Howard Cragin reached for his Bible and headed outdoors. Standing on a mound of dirt, he faced the frenzied crowd. He knew that the very life of his entire family was being threatened by this drunken horde. God was also at work. While the religious leaders had been instilling hatred in the minds of their followers, God had been building into the hearts of some of the people of Agato an appreciation for the compassionate "heretics" who bandaged their wounds, put salve on their burns and helped deliver their babies.

Rosa and her husband, Nicolas, were already definite converts. They, along with other sympathetic Indians, heard the approaching mob and hurriedly gathered together their own group to defend the Cragins. God was on their side, for what could have turned into a nasty confrontation gradually dissolved as the Otavalan crowd retreated.

Another uprising erupted three years later on May 29th, 1921. Once again the priest from down in Otavalo led the angry, half-drunken band of 150 or more. However, this time there were soldiers in the crowd who had been enlisted to produce even more fear.

As the group gathered in front of the Mission house, Howard Cragin took advantage of the opportunity and boldly preached Christ to them. Once again the mob retreated without major incident.

In the spring of 1921, George LeFevre came to join the Cragins in the work. How happy they were to have a reinforcement. But only four months after arriving in Agato, Lefevre contracted a deadly fever. Young George breathed his last on July 9th, 1921.

Howard Cragin tried to get permission to bury the body in the local cemetery. Permission was denied by the religious authorities who controlled the cemetery.

"His body would pollute our consecrated soil," they said.

Finally a carpenter was found who agreed to build a casket for the decaying body. A grave was dug in the front lawn of the Mission property. George's body was placed in the crude wooden box and lowered into the earth. It was a dark hour for the embryonic work of The Christian and Missionary Alliance in Imbabura.

Nicolas and Rosa's father also succumbed to the same dreaded fever. Their grief was accentuated by the fact that the religious leaders once again would not give burial permission. A grave was finally dug for him in his own small field.

Animosity intensified. Many Indians considered it a disgrace to have this "boil" (presence of the evangelicals) festering on the chest of Taita Imbabura. Some openly cursed the day the Cragins had arrived. The fledgling evangelical church in Agato irritated the feared, but not respected, religious leaders. But this embryo had been planted by God Himself. Slowly and painstakingly He was bringing together its parts. Although there would be desperate attempts to abort it, there would be no stopping the growth of this embryo.

Simultaneously, 4,000 miles to the north, God was knitting together another embryo in the womb of a woman who did not yet even know Him. The woman, Emma Reese Rychner (pronounced Rich-ner), desperately wanted a baby girl. She already had two boys whom she loved dearly, but it would be so much fun, she thought, to have a little girl around. Emma had not the slightest inkling that the God of heaven planned to use the tiny, developing embryo in her womb in ways that would be eternally significant.

Suppose you had been God. Suppose you knew, as He did, all you planned to accomplish through this little life your fingers were knitting together.

Suppose your mind leaped into the future and you realized that one day you would transplant this person into lofty, thin-aired territory high in the Andes—a territory virtually controlled by Satan and his wretched demons.

Suppose you were to meditate upon the assignment to the arduous task of transforming the heart of Imbabura into a symbol of your love. Suppose you pondered the difficulty of turning a rainbow inside out, defeating the powerful forces of hell itself and helping to establish a significant, aggressive, living church. What kind of child would you elect to make?

With a flair of infinite, beautiful wisdom, and perhaps even in defiance of man's puny thought processes, God's nimble fingers selected two Y chromosomes and declared with unchallengeable firmness, "It shall be a girl!"

Her parents named her Evelyn.

On February 4, 1919, God's achievements in Pierz, Minnesota, and in Agato, Ecuador, were no doubt linked in His own mind. Two embryos were now breathing and moving. One day He would weave the exquisite tapestry of His eternal purposes both for a baby girl in Minnesota, North America and for a baby church among the high-mountain Quichua Indians in the province of Imbabura, South America.

Strange, isn't it? Siamese twins are joined when they are born and are surgically separated afterward. These twins were separated by 4,000 miles at birth and joined 31 and a half years later.

2

The Making of a Servant

In 1932, Evelyn finished grade school in a little-house-on-the-prairie-style, one-room school. There were 30 children in all eight grades, but only one teacher. Evelyn was already in her early teens when people from the little mission church at the crossroads dropped by to invite the Rychner family to church.

"It's too far for us to come," Evelyn's father said. Mr. Rychner was right. It was six miles to the little church, a formidable distance in the 1930s.

The visitors from the church had an alternative proposal. Would Mr. Rychner, as a school board member, allow them to start a Sunday school in the school house?

It was all right with him, he said, but he couldn't speak for the other board members. Some were Catholic and he doubted they would approve of a Protestant church coming to the community. However, to everyone's surprise, the board unanimously agreed to allow the group to hold services in the school.

Pastor Clarence Swanson, a Covenant pastor, led the Sunday meetings. Evelyn began to attend.

The following summer, a Vacation Bible School was conducted in the nearby Swedish community of Freedhem. Once again two women came to the farm to ask if the Rychner children could attend. Evelyn's father agreed, but only after the women promised to send a car to pick them up.

One day at the meetings, in response to the invitation to receive Christ, Evelyn raised her hand. Her brother Edwin, who was sitting beside her, poked her in the ribs.

"There could be trouble at home!" he warned.

Evelyn did it anyway. In her own words, she was "thoroughly converted." Her life changed dramatically. Hers was no half-hearted commitment. Even then, in her early teens, Evelyn threw herself unreservedly into serving the Lord.

One by one every member of Evelyn's family came to Christ. God changed a pagan Minnesota family into a dedicated, supportive group who would one day commit themselves to stand solidly behind Evelyn in the years of her ministry that followed.

The consuming desire of Evelyn's heart was to reach others for Christ. Her attempts to witness did not satisfy her. She felt so inadequate.

Willis Alfors, the student pastor at the little church, suggested that Evelyn might benefit from attending Bible school. But how, she wondered, could she get there earning only $2.50 a week doing housekeeping?

An opportunity came for Evelyn to work as a maid for a family in Evanston, Illinois. There she received $8.00 a week plus room and board. Within one year Evelyn had saved enough to pay for her tuition at the St. Paul Bible Institute (now Crown College).

It was while Evelyn was in her third year at St. Paul that the Rev. Alexander Kowles, a missionary to China, came to Simpson Memorial Church as speaker for the annual missionary convention. He challenged the students to invest their lives in reaching the lost around the world. That night Evelyn dedicated her life to God, not only to reach the lost, but specifically the lost among the high mountain people of South America.

Within days Evelyn submitted her application for missionary service to The Christian and Missionary Alliance. The process would turn out to be a testing both of Evelyn's patience and her commitment.

The response to her application, when it finally came, was not the one Evelyn wanted or expected. There was no way, the letter said, that she would be accepted for foreign service without a high school diploma.

Evelyn was somewhat incensed. Why, she

had taken an extra year at St. Paul in order to qualify for further studies. Didn't that count for anything? And after all, she *had* graduated from a Bible school. Why hadn't they told her when she enrolled at the Institute that this training would not be enough? It was, for Evelyn, a disturbing turn of events.

Evelyn went to Ruth Jones, an Institute teacher whom she highly respected. Wisely, Miss Jones counseled her, "Evelyn, you can't look back. You have to go forward."

Evelyn decided to acknowledge God's sovereignty. She went ahead with her plans to minister that summer in Montana with Sue Schmidt, another St. Paul student. She and Sue had sung together as part of their Christian service assignment at the school. The ministry of the summer was enjoyable and fulfilling, an encouragement to Evelyn's somewhat discouraged heart.

Evelyn tried to complete high school by correspondence, but she found algebra too difficult. About at the point of desperation once again, she heard that the University of Minnesota offered courses leading to a high school diploma. She enrolled in the nursing course, with some electives in typing, bookkeeping and office practice. How could Evelyn foresee then that not one of those skills would be wasted in Imbabura?

In 1945, Evelyn finally earned her high school diploma. With that behind her, the major obstacle to Evelyn's vision of getting to the high mountains of South America no longer existed. However, another hurdle lay directly ahead. It was the requirement that all missionaries of The Christian and Missionary Alliance had to take at least one year at the Missionary Training Institute at Nyack, NY. So, once more, Evelyn was off to school—this time to Nyack.

Through all these unpredictable turns in her life Evelyn was learning valuable lessons that would benefit her in the future. It was a preparation custom-made to mold Evelyn Rychner into a servant of the Lord with a heart for Imbabura.

3

The Obstacle Course

After all the educational requirements had been fulfilled, Evelyn's application to The Christian and Missionary Alliance was once again reviewed. A letter dated March 25, 1946, read:

> *Your name has been reviewed in the recent meetings of the Bureau, Foreign Department, and Board and you are listed as an accredited candidate. This means that we do not require further education before appointment.*
>
> *You should be engaged in some kind of soul-saving ministry in the homeland while you wait for further word from us. It should be with a feeling that your work is the highest plan of God for you, and you should pursue it as if your whole life were to be spent in that way. It may be.*
>
> *Be sure to make good in the home ser-*

*vice. See souls won to the Lord. Learn to
pray through your problems and get spiritual victories and success in your work. If
you are a failure at home, there is no
reason to feel that a passport will so
change you as to make you a success
abroad.*

    *May the blessing of the Lord be upon
you.*

    Sincerely yours,
    W.F. Smalley
    Personnel Secretary

Evelyn headed for the Texas/Mexican border to fulfill her home service requirement.
Every clickety-clack of the train's wheels on
the segmented tracks signaled another step
away from the familiar surroundings of home
and another step toward her destiny. She was
alone—alone with her thoughts and her battered
wooden trunk. That trunk! It would be her
silent companion for the next 40 years.

The year was 1946. The national economy
was not the best. Evelyn's personal economy
was even worse. By man's standards it was a
disaster. She had managed to pull together
enough money to get to South Texas, but there
was no money or promise of money for rent,
food or anything else for that matter.

It wasn't until after Evelyn arrived in the
McAllen/Pharr area of the Rio Grande Valley
that she received a letter from her home church

promising $10 a month support. That was the first indication of how she would make ends meet. Later, the amount was increased to $20, a sum that was enough, with careful budgeting, for food for one person.

Rent was another matter. Each month's end became an "exciting" adventure in faith for Evelyn. One month, when it came time to pay the rent, Evelyn counted out her available funds. She still lacked $5.00, a considerable sum in 1946. That same day the mail brought a letter from a lady who normally sent her $1.00 each month. This time, however, the envelope contained $5.00 and a brief explanation: "I was saving this to buy a bedspread," the note said, "but the Lord revealed to me that you had a need. I want you to use this money wherever it is needed."

After several months in Texas, Evelyn received a letter from the headquarters of The Christian and Missionary Alliance in New York City. It informed her that her name had been put up for appointment and that she would likely be going to Colombia or Chile. Evelyn was very pleased. From that day on she watched the mailbox eagerly—week after week, month after month. Nothing came.

When the second letter finally arrived—one year later—Evelyn was asked if she would be willing to serve in Ecuador.

"Certainly," she responded. "Any Latin American country would be wonderful!"

"Village work with Miss Rosalie Roble on the coast" was the assignment. Evelyn would be expected to conduct Vacation Bible Schools, do visitation and hold evening meetings. Having already had training and experience in all of those areas, Evelyn was ecstatic.

She began to correspond with Irene Downing, a single missionary who had served in Ecuador for 24 years. One letter from Irene listed items Evelyn should try to bring with her: a good bed, a rolling pin, kitchen knives, waxed paper, sifters, strainers, dishpans, mixing bowls, serving bowls, birthday cards, wrapping paper and ribbon, a tea kettle, a coffee pot and plenty of shoes and stockings.

"A few paper napkins are nice to have, too," Irene wrote, "and don't think, as some of us have in the past, that because you are coming to the mission field that you must renounce all things pretty. . . ."

Then Irene added: "If you bring along a good sense of humor and the ability to get along with your fellow missionaries, you can dispense with a lot of the other equipment mentioned." What wise counsel this would turn out to be!

The language barrier, even in Texas, was extremely frustrating. But it was the motivation Evelyn needed. She hired a lady to teach her Spanish. It was a long and laborious process, but perseverance finally paid off and Evelyn was able to communicate effectively.

Evelyn felt a particular burden for the wetbacks, so called because they had gained entrance to the United States illegally by swimming the Rio Grande River. Many were won to Christ.

They began to meet for worship in an old sheep barn. But, as people were saved and the congregation grew, the need for a church building became apparent. To raise funds, Evelyn and her colleagues collected and sold used clothing. Soon they had enough money to buy a piece of land and by faith they began to construct a church to seat 200. Before Evelyn left the Mexican border, the walls were up, the roof was in place, the windows were installed and even a bell occupied the belfry.

Another bell, in another place, would one day have even more significance.

4

Ecuador at Last!

The few days at headquarters in New York City passed swiftly. There were numerous last minute experiences: a visit to Dr. Weddigen for final medical clearance, a commissioning service with the laying on of hands by the headquarters personnel, the gathering together of the missionary shipmates.

Evelyn and Marian Bucher shared a compact stateroom for the 10-day voyage aboard the block-long *Margarita*, a Grace Line passenger/freighter. John and Mary Bucher and their baby son, Paul, were also a part of the group. So were Mr. and Mrs. Paul Roffe who were returning to Peru. Some Methodist missionaries completed the contingent.

After the novelty of the vastness of the ocean and the details of the ship wore off, there was not a lot to do on board except rest. And rest was just what Evelyn needed. Those final days of packing and farewelling and deciding what to take as well as what not to take had been hectic. She needed these days of mental and physical restoration as a preparation for ministry in her adopted country.

One day, with Marian Bucher asleep on her narrow, cot-like bed in their stateroom on one of the lower decks, Evelyn slipped out. She wanted to breathe in the cool air and enjoy the spaciousness of the sky. She wanted to feel the ocean breezes sting her face. She wanted to smell the salt water.

She glanced at the glassy sea and felt a surge of gratitude. She had not relished the thought of seasickness. John Bucher had advised, "Keep your stomach full and you will not get seasick!" So far it had worked. The penalty would be a gain of five pounds during those 10 days.

The serendipity of seeing a dolphin break the surface of the water caught Evelyn's attention. The sleek, gray body came entirely out of the water and re-entered gracefully with a gentle, rolling motion. It was nice, she thought, to be free of responsibilities and not to have to think about how long she lingered there.

Only a few persons were on the sundeck at the moment. Ordinarily a gregarious person such as Evelyn would bemoan the absence of people to talk to. Today, however, she felt an uncharacteristic surge of gratefulness for the solitude.

The deck chairs were close to one another, like most everything on board ship. With a for-no-particular-reason deep sigh, Evelyn sank into a sagging chaise lounge. *People look more comfortable in these things than they feel!* she noted wryly to herself.

Evelyn's thoughts replayed the events of the days immediately behind her—the days together with her mother in Texas: packing her one steamer trunk and one suitcase; the two wooden boxes full of books and literature (even the boxes themselves would later be used for bookcases); the used kerosene refrigerator deliberately packed in a box that could become her table; the second-hand bed and a few commentaries that completed her meager outfit.

Evelyn could still see her mother at the train station crying. Brother Phil, too, had tears in his eyes.

She thought of the car trip from Williamsport, Pennsylvania, to New York City with Velma Green, her brother and her parents. Evelyn had driven all the way—it would be good practice for driving in Ecuador, her passengers noted half-joking, half-serious. Their observations would prove to be more accurate than they knew.

A spray of salt water hit her face. Yes, life would be radically different in Ecuador. Among other things, there would be little or no opportunity to meet a prospective mate there. Her colleagues for the most part would be married couples and single women. Not many men went to the mission field single. When they did, the competition was fierce!

Evelyn had never looked upon marriage as an essential to fulfillment. Oh, there had been young men who had shown an interest. She was a fun-loving person and those dating experiences had been enjoyable. The balance between wholesome Christian fun and serious spiritual discussion had been good. Happy memories were deposited in her memory bank that time could never erase.

The problem was that the young men had been more interested in her than in missions. Her commitment to God was definite. Nothing and no one would ever stand in the way of her call to the mission field. Too often she had watched a girl with a "call" become interested in a fellow who had none and had seen her opt in favor of the new love. By God's grace Evelyn had determined that that would never happen to her.

Slumped in the deck chair aboard *The Margarita*, how could Evelyn possibly know that waiting at the end of the voyage was a young man very eager for marriage?

The days on board ship slipped by altogether too quickly. In some ways Evelyn wanted them to go on forever. In other ways, she felt an inner excitement about the new experiences ahead.

At Guayaquil (pronounced Gwy-ah-keel⁻), Ecuador's largest city, the larger ships could not navigate the shallow Guayas River, so *The Margarita* docked at Puna Island. Evelyn and Marian stood at the rail, straining for a glimpse of Charles Eamigh, the newly-elected field chairman. What they didn't know was that the annual conference was underway up in the capital city of Quito (pronounced Key´-toe). In his place, the field chairman sent Miss Ethel Fetterly, known as "Queen" to many because of her statuesque bearing, to meet the new arrivals. Miss Fetterly gracefully ascended the gangplank and lovingly embraced Evelyn and Marian. Together they boarded *The Rosita*, the Grace Line's launch that would carry them through the bay and up the river to the landing pier.

Guayaquil had a repugnant reputation for thievery. Evelyn and Marian were warned to hide their wrist watches and to clutch their purses securely under their arms. The very warning added an aura of fear to the steamy atmosphere.

From the dock to the guest house was only a matter of minutes. The guest house was run by the straight-laced Rosalie Roble with whom Evelyn was destined to travel and minister during her first term. But that's another story.

5

Temporary Detour

The assignment as originally given by the New York office had been to work with Miss Roble traveling among the coastal villages, to conduct Vacation Bible Schools and to conduct meetings in the churches.

However, the Rev. Miguel Lecaro, who pastored the large Guayaquil Temple, was pleased that Evelyn and Marian Bucher were both already fluent in Spanish when they arrived. He immediately incorporated them into the ministry of the Temple and assigned them to visitation in homes and assisting in the Sunday afternoon street meetings. He also asked Evelyn to play the organ at the new believers' classes where they were learning to sing the unfamiliar gospel songs.

Evelyn also busied herself with children's meetings. Her first attempt was a never-to-be-forgotten occasion. Under the shade of a tree in a beautiful and spacious backyard owned by one of the women from the church, Evelyn and a couple of the girls from the Temple set up benches, put up the flannelgraph board and tuned up the guitar.

Evelyn suggested that the petite Azucena and her friend take a cowbell and walk through the nearby streets ringing it. It would announce that the Vacation Bible School was about to begin and would encourage the neighborhood children to attend.

"Oh no, Señorita!" Azucena replied. "We can't do that!"

"What do you mean, you can't do that?" Evelyn asked. "Why, there's nothing to it!"

But both girls insisted that they simply could not do it.

"All right, then," replied Evelyn in her usual enthusiastic manner, "I'll do it myself."

And she did.

Soon the backyard was filled with a large group of excited niños (children). When Evelyn returned from her bell-ringing expedition, the girls were grinning from ear to ear.

"How many people came running out with their garbage?" they asked, giggling self-consciously.

What Evelyn did not know was that only the garbage man came through the streets ringing a cowbell! The cowbell, however, had served its purpose for this time. Next time, Evelyn would know better.

It soon became apparent that a young Ecuadorian named Pascual Molina had his eye on Miss Rychner. It was obvious that he wanted to be around her as much as possible. Oh, he was a Christian and active in the Lord's service, but he was overly attentive and Evelyn felt uncomfortable around him. Her genuinely bubbly personality was accepted by other nationals without their interpreting it as flirting. With Pascual it was different. She hardly dared be even mildly friendly toward him.

Pascual's reputation was already well established. His goal, clearly and publicly stated, was to marry an American and he was determined that nothing was going to hinder him from achieving that goal. Evelyn was just one in a string of many American women who had been the object of his devoted but annoying attention. Even the reserved Miss Roble had been on his list of prospects.

Evelyn tried to tell Pascual as graciously and then as firmly as possible that she was not interested. Pascual persisted.

Perhaps if an older missionary man were to talk to Pascual, it would make a difference, Evelyn thought to herself. Paul Young was one of the most highly respected men in the missionary community. He was also a very gracious, gentlemanly person, which added even more to his stature.

Evelyn approached Paul and explained how annoying Pascual was becoming. She would appreciate it if he could make the man understand that she had a ministry to perform and was not at all interested in romantic involvement with him.

In spite of the graciousness of Paul's exhortation, Pascual took it poorly. He became very angry and threatened to see to it that all missionaries would be forced to leave the country. He did, however, leave Evelyn alone after that.

It was not to be the last time a man would show an interest in Evelyn. The next time, it would be so different.

6

Miss Roble

Miss Roble! To this day her memory revives an impressive array of emotions: admiration, appreciation, respect. A dedicated missionary with a dynamic teaching ministry, Rosalie Roble was certainly deserving of all those things and more.

As a young woman, Rosalie Roble had persisted in her desire to serve the Lord even though she was disowned by her family when she converted from Catholicism. Her family had tried to place her in a convent. Instead, someone at Toccoa Falls College in Georgia took her in and Rosalie eventually found herself in Ecuador.

Although Evelyn admired her greatly, not everyone got along well with Miss Roble. Her penchant for offering unsolicited advice, combined with a somewhat abrasive personality, simply rubbed some people the wrong way. Some described Miss Roble's demeanor as self-assured. Others, less charitably, called it overbearing. It was this very tall, very prim and very proper senior missionary that was to become Evelyn's traveling companion for most of her first year on the field.

Evelyn got along fine with Rosalie. People are all different from one another in their own ways, was Evelyn's philosophy. You just have to give them room to be themselves. You have to give them the liberties they need. If they infringe a little bit upon you, well, that's all right, too.

But life with Miss Roble would not be easy. The first confrontation came as Evelyn's first Christmas in Ecuador approached.

Evelyn had been invited to spend Christmas with some friends in the capital city, Quito. Although Quito was on the equator, it had an altitude of nearly two miles. The days would be cool and the nights so chilly that blankets would be welcome. It would be refreshing for Evelyn to get away from the oppressive heat of the coast. It would also be fun to be with some less "proper" folks with whom she would not be afraid to be the vivacious, bubbly person she really was.

Evelyn broached the subject with Miss Roble. Rosalie stiffened noticeably. That surprised Evelyn, for Miss Roble gave the impression that stiffening was perpetual and thus not possible upon occasion!

"Oh, Evelyn," Miss Roble replied, stiffening still intact. "How can you do that? I have a trip planned out to La Bocana on the coast. I'm always there at Christmas helping them with their Christmas program. They will be expecting me. It will not be possible, then, of course, for you to go to Quito."

The "of course," it seemed, settled it once and for all, at least in Miss Roble's mind.

Evelyn accepted the verdict without voicing the inner disappointment she felt. *After all,* she reasoned, *I am just a new missionary. I will do what I am told.*

Lord Jesus, she prayed silently, *I would love to celebrate Christmas in Quito with my friends, but I came here to serve You and I will trust You to make this a very special Christmas in Your own way.*

The long journey to La Bocana began on a river boat at night. Rosalie and Evelyn had two hammocks secured for them in the hopes of getting some sleep on the dangerously over-crowded vessel. Perhaps the word "secured" is a poor choice, for the hammocks swung precari-ously toward the open edge of the boat with each roll of the waves. It was anything but secure and Evelyn feared she might be tossed out into the swift current at any moment.

When they reached port, the women trans-ferred from the rickety boat to a rickety truck-turned-bus packed with live chickens, produce, crude baggage, multitudes of local peasants and the two furtively-stared-at gringas. Evelyn repressed a chuckle as she thought of what the two of them must look like to the Ecuadorians—especially the erect and rigid Rosalie Roble who towered head and shoulders above them all, including Evelyn.

No one was there to meet the bus in La Bocana. The irregularity of arrival times made that a virtual impossibility. Undaunted, Miss Roble recruited two little, brown-skinned boys with exceptionally bright, dark eyes and shiny black hair to help carry their paraphernalia to the church. Believers began to appear from nowhere.

There was the customary round of greetings and the girls were informed that they would be staying in an empty, one-room, bamboo house that squatted by the church. The loving hands of the believers had cleared the place of dust, dirt, ants, salamanders and assorted debris. Evelyn noticed a huge, furry tarantula under the overhang of the roof. Already she had learned that older missionaries didn't think anything of that. The stories of their poisonous bites were greatly exaggerated, they claimed, and besides, tarantulas were very good at catching insects. With a shiver Evelyn turned away from it. Harmless or not, she doubted she would ever feel comfortable sharing a home with those furry creatures. Now the extremely poisonous exis snakes were another matter. Even seasoned missionaries were afraid of them!

"You must inquire about the beginnings of this church, Evelyn, my dear," Rosalie advised. "The story is really quite amazing."

Señor Piedra seemed pleased to comply with Evelyn's request to relate the story. In a soft, earnest voice he recounted the following:

"A man came into our area looking for work. He appeared undernourished, almost sickly. I really didn't have any job on my fruit farm to offer him, but I took pity on him and said, 'Well, I could use you for awhile.' The man was with me for about a month until he became rather seriously ill and had to return to Guayaquil. He left a small cardboard box with me, securely tied with rope, which contained his meager possessions.

"Time passed and he did not return. We thought maybe he had died, so I opened up the little box. I noticed a small booklet. I couldn't read, so I called for my wife. She read some of it.

" 'Oh!' she exclaimed, 'This is a gospel!' We both knew that was a booklet the evangelicals used.

"Together we studied it. My wife would read and I would listen eagerly. We began to invite our neighbors in so they could hear her read, too. They were also very interested. We wondered if there were more books like this one. It warmed our hearts. We liked it.

"I became so hungry to learn more that I made a trip to Guayaquil and found the Alliance Temple where Dr. Miguel Lecaro was pastor. It was a big, beautiful building. A man was there cleaning the church. I showed him the little booklet that we had been studying.

" 'Are there more of these books?' I asked.

" 'Yes,' he said, 'There is a whole Bible!'

"I was so glad that I had taken enough money along with me. I bought the Bible and carried it back with me to El Oro. My wife began the reading sessions again and the neighbors came too.

"We listened to the story of creation with great interest. When my wife came to the Ten Commandments, I was amazed to hear, 'You shall have no other gods before me. You shall make no graven images.'

"I said, 'Listen to that! In all our homes we have an altar with many images. We've got to get rid of them.'

"My neighbors said, 'Oh, no! If we do that something terrible will happen to us.'

"I said, 'If we do not do this, the Bible says we will be punished down to the fourth and fifth generation. I'm going to do it! I'm going to get rid of my graven images.'

"Even my wife begged me not to, but I did it anyway. I wanted to obey God. Now nobody would come for our reading times. They were all afraid. They watched to see what terrible thing would happen to me and my family. Nothing happened. Slowly, one by one, they started coming back. The Bible continued to feed our souls.

"We learned from God's Word without a missionary or anyone else to help us but the Holy Spirit. By the time the first missionary came into our area, we had already built our little church and were tithing our earnings. God, through His Word, had taught us."

Evelyn found the story fascinating. *Just think,* she thought to herself, *I am participating in a Christmas celebration at a church that God Himself started!* This Christmas was turning out to be a special one after all.

Another confrontation with Miss Roble was not long in coming.

Evelyn was a pragmatist. She detested the length of time it took to care for her long hair. She also disliked the sticky, clinging feel of it against her perspiring neck. When Mrs. Reed, one of the ladies at the Temple, offered to cut it for her, Evelyn was delighted.

"Oh," she exclaimed, her voice rising to that higher pitch so characteristic of her when she was excited, "that would be wonderful!"

And it *was* wonderful—in everyone's eyes except Miss Roble's.

"Evelyn, my dear," Rosalie scolded, "why did you ever do a thing like that? I don't see how I can travel with you in the province. Why, people are just going to . . . they are not going to know what to think. Everybody wears long hair. I simply cannot have you looking like that."

It isn't really short, it's just shorter, Evelyn's mind retorted, but she opted to hold her tongue.

"Well, there isn't a lot I can do about it now," Evelyn finally replied, "except to let it grow back, and that will take some time."

Although it was uncharacteristic for Miss Roble to swallow anything, she managed to swallow her embarrassment at the looks of young Evelyn and the dark thoughts about "the worldliness of the new arrivals on the field these days!" She continued to take Evelyn along, in spite of her "outrageous" looks.

Naranjito. How could Evelyn ever forget that town? It was the custom for the girls to hand out tracts whenever they entered a settlement. At Naranjito, where Evelyn had gone alone, the tracts were not well received. Instead, a mob began to assemble and Evelyn soon found herself the focal point of a rapidly deteriorating situation. Right before the missionary's eyes, the people tore up all the tracts they could find and threw them to the ground in a display of obvious hatred and repulsion. They demanded that the "protestant virgin" leave town. Thankfully, the local lay leader intervened and Evelyn was allowed to continue to hold meetings, protected by the constitution. That constitution! It would be the basis of appeal on numerous occasions throughout Evelyn's years in Ecuador.

But Naranjito was memorable for another reason as well. It was there that Evelyn committed one of the grandest linguistic faux pas of her career.

The first night of the meetings (after the confrontation with the mob), Evelyn got up to give Miss Roble's greetings to the group. She began by explaining that Rosalie had not been able to accompany her on this trip.

"La Señorita Rosalia está para ir a los Estados Unidos," she said, or so she thought. The translation of what she thought she said was, "Miss Roble is about to go to the United States."

Without realizing it, Evelyn had slurred "está para ir" into "está parir."

The local pastor and Laura Hidalgo, with whom Evelyn was traveling, began to snicker uncontrollably. Ignoring them, Evelyn carried on.

After the service she asked, "What did I say that was so funny?"

"You said Miss Roble was going to the States to have a baby and you used the word for animals giving birth!"

The misstatement stimulated some rather curious mental pictures.

The prim and proper Miss Roble?

Fifty years old and single?

About to have a baby?

A most unlikely event on all accounts!

7

A Mountain
with a Heart

Freedhem, Minnesota. You don't need a
lengthy description of Freedhem. Actually,
there isn't much to tell. It boasted two
churches. One of them was Lutheran and the
other was a Mission church. A general store, a
creamery and a little school that provided classes only through eighth grade completed the
architectural roster. There were also dairy farms
where families eked out a simple existence,
always hoping for better times.

Imbabura. A description of Imbabura? Yes,
you do need a description of Imbabura. But you
won't like it.

Imbabura Province peaks and valleys itself
around the base of a massive mountain which
dominates the landscape. Ordinarily, clouds
obscure its impressive peak. On rare occasions,
Mount Imbabura manages to unveil its face.
There is something about this Andes mountain that makes it unique: *it has a heart!* Its
slope is graced by a valentine-shaped clearing
and it is most striking (see cover painting taken

from actual photograph).

When that gigantic heart was etched out on its slopes, no one but God Himself knows.

A closer examination of the base of the heart solves the *how* of it. The rubble fanning out among the trees makes it clear that two terrifying landslides created this dramatic effect. Is it any wonder, then, that daily sacrifices are made to Taita Imbabura? The Otavalan Indians revere him. They fear him. They personify him. They respect him.

The patchwork quilt slopes of Imbabura could tell the tales of wives squatting by the fallen bodies of alcoholic husbands too drunk to make it home, patiently awaiting their return to consciousness. They could tell of a child left there as a guard, for without protection the inebriated would be stripped naked of every stitch of clothing from his unconscious body. Tomorrow it could be the wife's turn to drink herself into oblivion. Then the husband would stand guard over her.

The Indians became intoxicated regularly. When a new baby was registered, they drank heavily. When a house was being built, they indulged in the fiery sugar cane rum at every turn of a corner in the mud walls. When a young person became a teenager, they all drank. When an Indian returned from a successful business trip, he threw a "Festivity of Prestige" party where the guests would become thoroughly inebriated on the liquor he provided.

The prestige gained was his for having so generously provided liquor and food. Then, once a week—every Saturday—when the market transactions were completed, the Indians went to the cantinas to drink and drink and drink some more.

In addition, in Imbabura, thieves were greatly feared. At night, in their one-room, mudwalled, thatch-roofed houses, people slept lightly, with their wealth as close to their bodies as possible, for their thieves roamed everywhere. Some slept on their porches where they could more easily hear anyone trying to steal their crops or animals tethered close by.

The thieves did not always content themselves only with stealing. At times they beat people mercilessly, often wantonly mutilating and murdering.

Fear was ever present, too, but not only because of the thieves. There was also the rainbow. Men, women and children trembled in fear when a rainbow burst forth on a rainy/sunny afternoon. Everyone knew the rainbow was the symbol of the devil. The brighter its colors, the greater the terror it produced. The Indians beat on empty kettles or pinched the ears of their dogs to make them howl in the hopes that the evil spirit causing the rainbow would be frightened away. In Imbabura there was nothing more terrifying than the rainbow.

And then there were the Indians' enemies. Everyone had enemies both among their fellow

Indians and in the spirit realm. They would gather up the dust bearing the footprints of an enemy and cast that dust in their fire. This, they believed, would place a curse on the enemy. It was a way of getting revenge.

In the midst of pervasive fear, however, was magnificent beauty. This picturesque Andean high country was so photogenic that it could easily lure any photographer with *National Geographic* aspirations.

Imbabura was no pre-Adamic paradise, however, for Satan had succeeded in transforming it into a suburb of hell. Already, in the early 1900s, before missionaries had penetrated the area, the province of Imbabura was unquestionably Satan's stronghold. Oh, religion was there. Large, imposing churches with tall steeples dotted the landscape. The churches were filled with statues. There were plenty of saints inside the church, but few that walked the streets on the outside. Priests absolved the parishioners' many sins, but some wondered who absolved the sins of the priests, which were also many.

Thousands upon thousands of religious Indians were faithful devotees of the Virgin and of the saints. They hilariously celebrated each religious festival by carrying images through the streets, accompanied by bands, firecrackers, dancing, heavy drinking and much fighting. All in the name of religion.

The Festival of St. John traditionally climaxed

with a rock-throwing session between factions of the Church. The women gathered piles of stones and passed them to the men to throw at each other. The inevitable injuries sometimes resulted in death.

For a fee, any Indian could go to the church and have the name of an enemy placed before Saint Bernard, believed to be the saint who causes death. The Indians were firmly convinced of the terrible powers of San Bernardo. If someone in a family became gravely ill, a representative would go to the priest to inquire if that person's name was on the death list before the saint. The priest would search and "find" the name. For another fee, the name could be removed so that the sick person would not die.

Religion only added burdens. It did not relieve them. The giant burdens of produce which the Indians carried on their backs as they jogged along toward market were truly symbolic of the monstrous burdens they carried in their hearts. The only real difference was that they could put down the ones they carried on their backs to rest a while, but there was not so much as a temporary respite from the burdens on their hearts.

In addition to the fear of thieves, enemies and rainbows, the Indians lived in perpetual fear of sickness. There was no place to turn with their ailments. They were afraid to go to the hospital where the whites went, knowing full well that they were not welcome. Since Indians were considered worthless, there was no incentive for the doctors to achieve a cure. The horror stories that circulated among the Indians concerning the hospital down in Otavalo were many. Some were spurious, others quite authentic.

Remedies were extremely primitive. One of the most effective for "easing" pain was to take a branch of fire nettles (that cause intense burning) and beat the painful area with it. The resulting discomfort was so severe it overrode the intensity of the original pain.

If a child had prolonged diarrhea, certain herbs were mixed with urine and burnt matchsticks. If the baby didn't improve after drinking that horrible concoction, a brick would be heated and the baby seated on the hot brick. The child's screams were ignored as its bottom burned and blistered.

The mountain with a heart had no love for its inhabitants. It simply stood there presiding over its hapless populace, boasting a certain natural grandeur, but with no power to help those who worshiped it. Generations lived out their painful, fear-filled lives on its steep, comfortless slopes.

On rare occasions Taita Imbabura "fathered" a child. Any albino or any blond-haired, blue-eyed child (of an Indian woman) fathered by a Spanish landlord was in the Indians' minds unquestionably one of Taita Imbabura's children.

Yes, Satan had certainly laid claim to Imbabura. His reign was ruthless and cruel. It was he who had twisted the rainbow—a symbol of God's glorious promise—into a terrifying instrument of fear and oppression.

When superstitions and fears and demons and hell have uncontested control, as they did in Imbabura Province, what does it take to break such demonic chains? Can a missionary do it alone? Can a Mission organization ensure success? Or must God Himself come down to the territory that has been wrested from His control by Satan and his cohorts?

And if God comes, in what form does He come? Through whom?

Surely a miracle would be required before that great heart on the chest of Taita Imbabura would come to symbolize something beautiful and something good, instead of something cruel and foreboding.

8

Bittersweet Ending

It was still Evelyn's first term of service and already she had had four different ministry assignments. First, she had worked with Dr. Lecaro at the church in Guayaquil. Second came the memorable itineraries with Miss Roble. Then, when Grace Morrison needed a break from teaching at the Women's Bible Institute in Los Cerros, Evelyn filled in. The bright spot in that ministry was that she was able to be with Marian once again.

Hardly had Evelyn completed that assignment when she was asked to manage the Alliance Bookstore in Quito. The Mission needed a replacement for Grace Shepherd who had been struck by a car and seriously injured.

And now, it was conference time and new assignments would be made—for Evelyn, her fifth in as many years.

Evelyn and Marian were asked to go to Agato to oversee the work among the Otavalan Indians. The Carlsons, now the resident missionaries in Agato, were going home on furlough. The women would be alone on the isolated Mission station on the slopes of Taita

Imbabura, four miles from the town of Otavalo. There would be no vehicle, no electric lights, no generating plant. Evelyn's training in practical nursing would come in handy at the clinic which was held regularly on the station. The office procedures course she had taken at the University of Minnesota would be helpful in keeping the Mission books. Farm life as a youngster on the homestead would simplify the rigors of the crude facilities. Evelyn remembered the byword of the St. Paul Bible Institute, "There are prepared places for prepared people." Surely God had prepared her for this new assignment.

Going to Agato, however, meant learning another language. In her heart Evelyn felt some rebellion. Having conquered Spanish, she would now begin yet another linguistic struggle, this time with Quichua.

At the time of the assignment, it didn't cross Evelyn's mind that the Carlsons might never return. No one realized then that Mr. Carlson's various signs of physical and mental deterioration were the onset of Alzheimer's disease.

Fellow missionaries respected this tall, thin man with the dry sense of humor. They knew how faithfully he had ridden his many-speeded English bicycle the four miles down from Agato into Otavalo to be a witness there. He was almost always present for the Saturday morning Indian market.

In addition, Carl Carlson had walked or ridden his bike all over the province of Imbabura. His Bible story chart was always with him. He told the gospel story to all who would stop to listen. At times he had been pelted with rotten fruit or worse, but he graciously endured those expressions of animosity and, in the process, gained the respect of many of the Indians.

As Evelyn arrived at the Agato compound and stepped through the lattice gateway, there, before her, stood an elderly Indian woman with graying hair. She was very slight of build and had a most winsome smile. With her hands clasped beneath her chin in an attitude of prayer, she welcomed Evelyn to the station.

"Oh, my precious Lord," she began to pray out loud, "bless this dear new missionary who has come to bring the gospel message." Her prayer was simple and sweet and sincere. That prayer was Evelyn's introduction to Mama Manuela (pronounced Mahn-weh´-lah).

Mama Manuela was one of the most devout of all the Indians in the Agato area. There had been a time when Mama Manuela was known for her foul mouth. She had cooked for pagan festivities and as the drinking progressed and the party got rougher, so did Manuela's language.

Mama Manuela was as afraid as anyone of the "devils" who lived in the Mission house on the slopes of Imbabura. She forbade her children to stop and talk with them. In fact, she urged them to hurry past so no curse would cling to them or afflict her household. After all, with her own ears she had heard the priest say that these foreigners were "devils who cause crop failure, contaminate the water and bring down divine wrath from heaven."

Manuela's son, Daniel, was not to be deterred by such stories. As a matter of fact, the rumors only aroused Daniel's curiosity all the more. When Mr. Carlson was working out in the front yard and Daniel passed by, there was always at least a brief conversation between them, initiated by the gregarious missionary who, along with his wife, Clara, had replaced the Cragins.

Daniel liked Mr. Carlson. He seemed genuine. If he were the devil he was purported to be, it would certainly have to be acknowledged that there was such a thing as a likeable devil.

One day, Daniel's sister became seriously ill. Mama Manuela tried everything she knew to cure her daughter. She burned candles before the Virgin. Certain that the eyes of the Virgin had looked upon her with compassion, Manuela was greatly encouraged until she realized that the little girl was no better.

Manuela carried her to the lake and bathed her in its icy water. That did not bring the fever down.

She sent some children, thought to be purer than adults, up the slopes of Taita Imbabura to offer a chicken to the spirit of the mountain in the hopes that it would be appeased. Josefa only worsened.

Daniel pled with his mother to take his sister to the Mission compound. "They have remedies there that work, Mama," he said. But Manuela would have nothing to do with those devils. Nothing!

Manuela visited the local witch doctor, but even the witch doctor was unable to help. He rubbed Josefa's body with a candle and then examined the candle long and hard. It revealed the cause of her illness, he said. He also rubbed the child's body with branches of medicinal herbs to concentrate the illness in one spot. Then he sucked on the spot, and, to Mama Manuela's amazement, produced a frog which, he said, he had sucked out. This was surely the cause of her daughter's illness. But that, too, had not helped.

In a neighboring community there was a witch doctor who was highly respected. One evening Manuela took Josefa to him. She made certain that she had everything with her that he required: a bottle of liquor, cigarettes, matches, candles, four eggs, red roses, carnations, and medicinal herbs from up on the slopes of Imbabura.

The witch doctor began by arranging an altar on the mud floor of the house. On a straw mat he laid out a pattern with his magic amulets. He spread out a woman's headcloth and sprinkled some rose and carnation petals on it. On each corner he placed one egg, some cigarettes and some herbs.

Mama Manuela sat fascinated as the witch doctor squatted behind the altar, his helper to his right and the fevered Josefa to his left.

The witch doctor put a spear in Josefa's hand so the evil spirits would see she was well-armed and would not attack her. He lit the candles and poured some of the liquor into a cup. He gave both his helper and Josefa a cigarette. Then he took one himself. Simultaneously they lit their cigarettes.

The brujo (pronounced brew´-ho; literal meaning—male witch) blew smoke in great gulps, making a sound like a strong wind and invoking the blessings of his mentor witch doctors in Santo Domingo de Los Colorados. He also called upon the power of Taita Imbabura and the power of the waterfalls.

Next he sipped a mouthful of liquor and spewed it out in a fine mist over the candles. The alcohol went up in flames and the hut glowed with the blue fire. It was electrifying! Mama Manuela was thrilled.

As the conjuring grew in intensity, suddenly the witch doctor leaned forward and, seizing two eggs, vigorously rubbed them over the back and chest of Josefa. The eggs would absorb the illness he said.

Finally the treatment was over. Ceremoniously, the witch doctor cleared the altar, folding the altar cloth carefully so no petals escaped. The helper would have to throw them way out into the darkness along with the eggs and the herbs. The witch doctor made a sign of the cross over the whole altar area and ordered Josefa to sleep on the folded altar cloth to ensure the success of the treatment.

Manuela and Josefa went home full of hope—unfounded hope, unfulfilled hope. Josefa only grew worse.

Manuela's neighbors suggested remedy after remedy. She tried them all. But neither Indian remedies, nor witchcraft, nor even the sacrifice of a chicken to Taita Imbabura made her daughter well.

One day, Daniel approached his mother, who by now was almost frantic.

"Mama, I have told you that down at the Mission house they have a clinic. They have remedies different from ours that are very powerful, even more powerful than the brujo's. I have seen some wonderful things happen there."

"Daniel! What were you doing there?" Manuela exploded. "That clinic is out behind the house where those devils live. Perhaps you have brought home this evil spirit that bothers your sister!"

"Mama, please," Daniel responded, "please try them. The witch doctors have not been able to help Josefa. On the front of the Mission house they have a sign that says, 'The blood of Jesus Christ cleanses from all sin.' I don't know all that means. Señor Carlson has tried to explain it to me. What I do know is that people get better quickly after they go to the clinic. The señor and señora both pray with the sick people who come to them. Their prayers are so different from the ones we hear down in the big church in Otavalo. Please, Mama!"

"Enough, Daniel, enough! I have heard enough! We will not take Josefa to these foreign devils. We will see what the witch doctor in Peguche can do. He recently took further training at Santo Domingo de Los Colorados and now everyone respects him even more. His fees are much higher, but perhaps he can help Josefa."

He couldn't. Josefa died.

Josefa's body was placed on a table-like platform and tied with ropes into a sitting position. An arch of branches and flowers was built over her body and candles were lit on either side of her.

Josefa had been baptized down in Otavalo. This guaranteed that she was immediately changed into an angel and went directly to heaven. Mama Manuela was supposed to find great comfort in the fact that her daughter was now in heaven interceding for her. Somehow though, as deeply ingrained as those teachings were, Manuela's spirit was not comforted. Her "liver shivered." Her head was "filled with little demons."

Josefa's body was placed in the simple wooden box built by the village carpenter and carried on the shoulders of friends to the consecrated ground in Otavalo. When they buried her it seemed to Mama Manuela as if all happiness and joy were buried with her.

Daniel watched his mother go deeper and deeper into depression. From time to time he brought up the subject of the Mission house, suggesting that Mama herself go there. But she was adamant in her refusal.

"Mama," he tried to assure her, "they have medicines for everything. I am sure they would have medicine for bad thoughts, too. Please go to them."

This time there was no outburst of indignation. In fact there was no answer at all. Perhaps the bad thoughts were overcoming her spirit completely.

A few days later Mama Manuela arrived at the Carlsons' door. Mrs. Carlson could hardly believe her eyes. She knew how strongly Manuela objected to their being there, yet here she was.

"Señora," Mama Manuela began, "I cannot get along with my thoughts as they are. Daniel tells me you have medicines that can drive away bad thoughts. Can you give me some of those medicines?"

"Oh, dear Mama," Clara Carlson said tenderly, "we do not have any medicines for you here at the clinic. I do have a remedy for you, though. I have a very dear Friend who can help you."

"Who is this friend?" Manuela inquired.

Clara told her simply about the Lord Jesus Christ, the Son of God, who loved her so much that He had even died for her. Mama listened intently to the gospel story.

"If He can help me," she said, "and will be my friend, and will take away these thoughts that are bothering me day and night, then I want to take Him as my Savior."

From that day Mama Manuela was transformed. She began to tell people everywhere about the Lord Jesus who was real and more powerful than any of their brujos, even the ones who had made the trip to Santo Domingo de Los Colorados.

Years later Mama Manuela testified: "I walked into this Mission station crippled, hunched over like an old, old woman. I walked out straight. God not only saved me, but He also gave me a new life. What God has done for me, I must tell the world. That is why I come to the clinic every day and tell the patients the good news while they wait for the nurse or doctor. I say, 'Here they have a remedy for your body, but I have a remedy for your soul. You must hear that first.'"

Manuela never did learn to read, but she memorized Bible stories and retold them thousands of times to anyone who would listen.

The ground floor of the large and somewhat spooky Mission house had two bedrooms off a hall that led from the living room/dining room area. With the Carlsons still packing for furlough, Evelyn and Marian temporarily shared the bedroom that was adjacent to the garage where their belongings were stored.

The first night in the house, Evelyn was awakened about midnight by a strange noise. It sounded like someone tapping or pounding. The noise of falling dirt immediately followed each tap and magnified to outrageous proportions in the inky blackness of the Ecuadorian night.

The sounds ceased as Evelyn stirred to awaken Marian. Since Marian had heard nothing, she dismissed the incident as understandable first-night jitters in this cavernous house. She went back to sleep.

Evelyn could not sleep. She just knew someone was out there in the garage. It had not been her imagination. She was sure of that. She lay there awhile. Then the faint tap, tap, tapping began again. The sound of falling dirt was unmistakable.

Evelyn quietly awakened Marian. Now Marian could hear the sounds, too. The two of them woke up Clara Carlson and together they searched for the key to the garage. Perhaps they could surprise the thieves in the very act.

With not so much as a squeak of the hinges, the women opened the front door of the house and hurried to the garage area. There was no one there! They could see where large mud bricks had been removed leaving a gaping hole in the wall. Apparently the thieves were wanting to make the hole big enough to carry out not only the suitcases, but other large household goods as well.

"Well," Clara Carlson said, "we can rest in peace. They will not be back now that they know they have been discovered."

The women replaced the mud bricks and went back to their rooms. It was not easy for Evelyn to get to sleep. This initiation to missionary life among the Indians had been somewhat disconcerting. Soon she and Marian would be living in this old house all alone. The thieves would no doubt return knowing that only two women were in the house and . . . .

But that story remains for the adventures of Evelyn's second term.

Evelyn once more launched into language study. It was a struggle. Quichua was a very difficult language to learn. She had done so well in Spanish, but this was different. Some words had 25 letters, with additional prefixes or suffixes possible. It was so frustrating that sometimes Evelyn despaired of ever learning what one missionary colleague called "probably the most difficult language on the South American continent."

It didn't help that Marian seemed to grasp Quichua much more easily than she, but Evelyn was no quitter. Difficult though the task was, she kept plodding. Friends were praying. Evelyn was working hard. Gradually, the Quichua language barricade was weakening. Little by little another obstacle to the sharing of the gospel finally yielded.

Then furlough time arrived.

9

Saved by the Bell

When Evelyn returned from furlough she was once again assigned to Agato, this time with Astrid Pearson. Evelyn was so delighted to be back in Imbabura Province that she requested that it be her permanent place of ministry, at least for her entire second term. She was convinced that she would accomplish little if she were once again a jack-of-all trades as she had been during her first term.

The Mission compound was an interesting place. It was girdled by a high, foreboding, chain-link fence which hopefully would keep robberies at a minimum. The addition of an electrical charge to the fence produced even more security, though certainly not an absolute guarantee. When the generator was shut down (as it was every night), of course the electrical charge also disappeared.

In the front yard of the compound, beneath a sprawling tree, a lone gravestone eloquently recalled the price of attempting to reach these people with the gospel. There could just as easily have been two graves there. Dr. V. Raymond Edman had come very close to join-

ing his colleague, George LeFevre. So close was
Dr. Edman to death that Mrs. Edman had dyed
her wedding dress black for the funeral and had
hired a carpenter to build the casket. But God
had other plans for Dr. Edman. (Dr. Edman
eventually became the president of Wheaton
College in Wheaton, Illinois.)

In addition to the solitary grave, there was the
ancient, two-story house with a bell hanging
under the peak of the eaves. The bell was used
to call the Indians to worship.

The compound also included a very small
chapel and a crude, but clean, two-room, lean-
to-type dispensary. A garden grew by the side
of the Mission house.

Between the garden and the dispensary squatted an open shed which housed the gasoline-
powered generator. What a welcome addition
that was! What an improvement over the primitive living conditions that the Cragins and
Carlsons had endured! Before the advent of
the generator there had been no light other
than candlelight and the flickering glow from
the fireplace in the living room of the Mission
house.

A path from the back mud fence, through the
tiny, well-kept fields of the industrious Otavalan
Indians, led up the slopes of Imbabura to a
place where sacrifices were made to the spirit of
Taita Imbabura.

After only one year in Agato, Astrid left to go
work among the Salasaca Indians, and Marjorie

Miller, a new missionary recruit, joined Evelyn in Imbabura Province.

Marge was a vivacious single woman with dedication plus. In many ways, Evelyn and Marge were much alike. Evelyn had an infectious chuckle; Marge laughed right out loud. Evelyn plodded steadily and energetically from early to late; Marge dashed with nervous energy from one task to another from almost as early to almost as late. Evelyn was known for her warm, sincere, enthusiastic hospitality (especially her famous rhubarb pie); Marge would one day entertain more missionary colleagues and other foreign guests than anyone in the history of the Mission.

Small wonder that Marge and Evelyn became life-long friends. There was no competition between them, though both vied for first place in the area of multiple involvements. Together they would weather many trials. One of those trials came early in their ministry in Agato.

Taita Rafael, the old Indian who helped Evelyn and Marge in the kitchen, had long since dried the last dish of the evening meal and had hung up his ragged blue denim apron on the hook that jutted from the kitchen wall.

"Hasta mañana!" he called softly into the dining room.

Later that evening, with Marge already drifting off to sleep, Evelyn headed out the back door, flashlight in hand, to shut off the generator. It was always a relief when the monotonous drone of the generating plant died down and silence prevailed.

Evelyn placed her notebook on the dining room table. She could work an hour or two yet by lamplight.

Within minutes, the Mission dogs interrupted her lesson preparation. *There they go again*, she thought, *breaking down the cornstalks*. She rose wearily and went out to tie them up so they would not damage the garden further.

Resuming her study, Evelyn noticed that the dogs were still agitated. This time she went to the window, leaned into the deep windowsill and shined her powerful, five-cell flashlight around the compound borders.

What she saw made her angry. Near the chicken yard and the rabbit hutch a hole had been knocked out in the mud wall. Thieves! She and Marge had been raising those rabbits and chickens for fresh meat.

Evelyn hurried out to let the dogs loose, but a few steps into the yard, she thought better of being out there alone and went back in the house. She decided that she would have a better vantage point upstairs.

Marge awakened to find Evelyn at an upstairs window peering into the night. It was dark, very dark. The only way to see anything would be to go back out into the yard.

"You are not going out there, Evelyn!" Marge snapped. "Why, they could attack you or kill you!"

Evelyn paused a moment. Marge was right. Only days earlier the mutilated body of one of the believers had been found rotting in a ditch after being attacked by thieves.

The fact that Evelyn had discovered the thieves did not frighten them. They stayed! They knew that there were only two defenseless señoritas living in the Mission house now. No man lived there. They had nothing to fear. They could do anything they pleased.

As Evelyn shined her flashlight out the upstairs window, a hunk of dirt smashed against the pane. Emboldened, the thieves began pelting chunks of dirt against the house.

"What shall we do?" Evelyn cried out as the seriousness of the situation became increasingly clear.

Suddenly, an idea flashed into her mind. Perhaps it was in answer to someone's prayer or to Evelyn's own silent plea. *The church bell! Yes, the church bell!* It hung under the eaves of the balcony on the second story.

Quickly Evelyn unbolted the door that opened out onto the balcony and pulled on the rope with all her might. The silence of the equatorial night, usually broken only by the barking of a skittish dog or the whining of the wind in the eucalyptus trees, was suddenly shattered. Indians sat bolt upright in their beds. They came running from every direction.

Taita Francisco was the first of many to arrive. Mama Manuela came through the hole the thieves had made in the mud fence. A group of men searched the grounds. They discovered that the thieves had taken all the chickens, but the rabbits had scurried into their holes and were safe.

Some of the men decided to stand watch through the night in the fields surrounding the Mission house. Huddled in little clusters for the protection numbers could provide, they would be ready if anyone decided to come back.

Mama Manuela came into the kitchen, knelt in the middle of the floor, placed her hands together beneath her chin and earnestly pleaded God's protection over her missionary friends. She, too, stayed all night, keeping her prayer vigil.

In addition to the insecurity of the situation at Agato, Evelyn and Marge were facing an even more worrisome reality. The truth of the matter was that only minimal spiritual results were being realized even though Evelyn and Marge were literally pouring out their lives in ministry to these Indians. If the answer to the ongoing, frustrating lack of fruitfulness in Agato were to be found in dedicated daybreak-to-moonlight effort, surely there would have been results. Finally, Evelyn could stand it no longer. Something had to be done.

"Marge," she said one day, "I've been thinking about when the Cragins first came to Agato.

They didn't live in this spacious house with a generator and a well and kitchen appliances and large rooms. They didn't drive a vehicle. They walked. They rented a mud hut with no windows and a straw roof and they lived just like the Indians did."

Evelyn paused momentarily as if to discern the effect her speech was having on Marge.

"I've been thinking about going up to Morochos to live. The Cumbas family would let me live with them. When Señora Cumbas was dying with complications following the birth of her child, I drove up to get her. I got stuck in the sandy riverbed and while we were getting the Land Rover out, they carried the señora on their backs like a gunny sack full of produce. I brought her back to Agato, but we couldn't help her here. I took her to Otavalo where she recovered in the hospital. She and her family feel that I saved her life and they are deeply appreciative. I just know they would let me live there."

Uncharacteristically, Marge said nothing, but Evelyn could tell by the look on her face that she did not think the idea was a good one.

"I could take a cot," Evelyn plunged ahead, "and live in their home. I could eat their food, walk their trails, share in their lives and show them that I don't feel I am above them."

With that, Marge finally exploded.

"No way! No way are you going to expose yourself to the lice, dirt and the germs that could bring you down with who knows what! That is not necessary. I would have to report your actions to the Mission committee if you decided to go through with a plan like that."

Evelyn backed off for the moment. But deep down, she still felt that this drastic step might be just what was needed to discover what made the Indian mind tick and what she should do to identify herself more closely with them.

A few nights after that conversation, Evelyn was reading before she retired. The flickering light of the kerosene lantern threw grotesque shadows on her bedroom walls and ceiling. But Evelyn didn't even notice. She was too fascinated by an article about an anthropologist named Rayburn. He had come to Ecuador to study the Quichua Indians and was making a trip into the mountainous interior dressed like an Indian.

The article told how Rayburn, along with an Indian guide, had registered at a tambo. Rain was dripping down onto their look-alike, rubberized ponchos from their look-alike hard felt hats. The mud walls of the inn's reception area seemed to absorb nine-tenths of the light from the struggling kerosene lantern. Rayburn was short, like his companion, and dressed exactly like him. They looked for all the world like two traveling Quichua men.

The lady at the desk greeted the guide with the customary Spanish phrase. Then she turned to Rayburn and said, "Buenas noches, mister."

Immediately Rayburn knew that she had rec-
ognized that he was a white man.

Later, in their room, Rayburn asked the
guide: "How could she possibly have known
that I was not an Indian?"

The Indian thought for a moment, and then
replied, "I guess it's because you don't have an
Indian mother."

The next day, Rayburn asked the receptionist,
"When I came in last night, I had every appear-
ance of being an Indian, yet you called me
'mister.' How did you know I was a white
man?"

The receptionist paused for a moment and
then replied, "You do not walk like an Indian."

Evelyn knew that Indians take little short
steps. They carry unbelievably heavy loads on
their backs—huge sheaves from the fields and
mammoth loads of assorted produce—to the
Saturday market. By jogging along the trails
with short steps, they are able to continue for
extended periods of time. This practice influ-
ences even their unburdened gait. By contrast,
Rayburn, like most North Americans, had taken
long strides.

Evelyn pondered the implications of the article for her own life.

There you have it, she said to herself. *I could
dress like the Indians, live like the Indians and eat
like the Indians, but my walk would betray me.
And if it weren't my walk, it would be something
else.*

That night Evelyn made a far-reaching decision—a decision between herself and God. That decision would probably more profoundly affect the future of the work in Imbabura Province than any carefully planned and diligently executed evangelism techniques or church growth principles.

I will do for the Indians, she determined, *whatever I would do for my fellow missionaries, my friends, and even my family members. If they ask for a ride, and I can possibly give it, I will. I will show them love and respect. I will go the second mile for them. I will demonstrate my love for them at all times. I will become to them a co-worker and not a "jefe"* (pronounced heff´-ay; boss). Evelyn never deviated from the deep commitment she made that night. Increasingly she was considered a co-worker by the Indian people she loved and served. Perhaps the Indians knew even before Evelyn did that she truly had *a heart for Imbabura.*

Meanwhile, Marge was concerned mainly for the Spanish (non-Indian) population of the area. In keeping with that burden, she worked with the church down in Otavalo. Services were conducted in a small corner store with chairs packed to the walls on each side of a narrow center aisle. The damp and dimly-lit facility did little to enhance the image of the evangelicals.

Marge arranged to bring in Dixie Dean from

Quito. He was a world-famous accordionist who had played before the Queen of England and was now serving with radio station HCJB. National pastors were engaged to do the preaching. Evelyn and Marge secured the town's main theater for the meetings. The campaign was a huge success.

At similar later campaigns, they pitched a large tent on an enclosed lot so the opposition could not tear it down. Unable to attack the physical facility, the priest broadcasted the names of people who were in danger of excommunication from the church if they persisted in attending the evangelical services. The people came anyway.

A spy from the factory also recorded names. One girl who attended told Evelyn that when she went to work the next morning her supervisor called her in to her office and asked, "Did you attend the service of the evangelicals last night?" She acknowledged that she had.

"Because you have told the truth, you will not lose your job," the supervisor responded, "but you should realize it is not good to go to evangelical meetings."

Over 50 persons signed decision cards at the end of one such campaign. When Evelyn and Marge did the follow-up, inviting the new converts to attend services in the evangelical store-front chapel, they encountered frightened people. One couple confided, "This is very difficult for us, señorita. We have a son studying for the priesthood."

In spite of the reticence of some to publicly associate themselves with the evangelicals, the storefront meeting room, which now housed both a Spanish and an Indian congregation, rapidly became too small. A piece of land was purchased on which to build a church. The new building that gradually took shape on the lot was impressive and did much to establish the permanence of the evangelical influence in Otavalo. The testimony to the community was strong—whites (Spanish descendants) and Indians working side by side with a common goal—to erect a beautiful edifice to the glory of God.

Marge taught English classes both in Agato at the Mission house and in the Cultural Center in Otavalo. In one of Marge's English classes there was a handsome, young medical doctor named Marcelo Endara. His mother owned a 27-room, Spanish-style home in the very heart of Otavalo. They were a wealthy and influential family.

Using the New Testament as her text, Marge taught Marcelo Endara English. The seed that was sown brought forth fruit when Marcelo confessed his faith in the Lord Jesus Christ. His conversion brought great joy to both Marge and Evelyn.

But Marcelo was developing another relationship as well—with Marge.

Marge and Marcelo Endara were united in

marriage on May 28, 1964.

The Mission had strict rules about mission-aries marrying nationals, so officially Marge was no longer considered a missionary. But Marge and Marcelo remained among Evelyn's greatest encouragers and dearest friends.

Marcelo inherited his mother's huge home. He and Marge renovated it and turned it into a hotel, complete with graceful Spanish arches opening to the central courtyard with its color-ful flower beds. The hotel, in addition to the hundreds of tourists who found it the only acceptable accommodation in Otavalo, hosted missionaries regularly. Thousands of meals were served in its impressive dining room. Marge took her place graciously among the upper class of the Spanish community in Otavalo.

Evelyn's turn for romance was still to come. But for now, her heart belonged only to Imbabura.

Evelyn Rychner, 1987. According to Evelyn, she "started out at five feet, three-quarter inches." Now she is just four feet, eleven and one-half inches.

Evelyn's family, taken after Nyack (about 1946). From left to right: Evelyn, Harvey, Edwin, Phil, Merle and Bernice, with Mother and Dad.

The Temple in Guayaquil. This church sponsors 54 street meetings per week and has mothered 14 other churches.

Taita Imbabura with its head covered by clouds.

Antonio Velasquez pointing to an area that has yet to be reached with the gospel.

Roast Cui (guinea pig). Cui is a must at any significant celebration. It was served at the dedication of the Agato church.

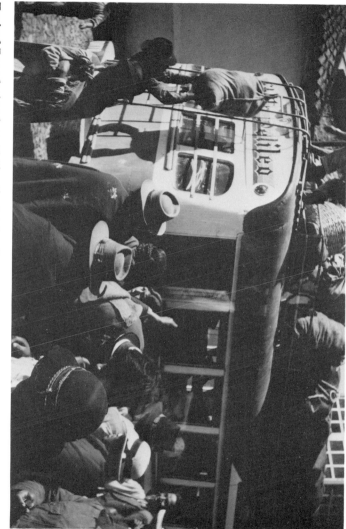

Typical Ecuadorian bus. Notice the top load.

A Quichua woman. As soon as baby girls are born, beads are placed around their necks. The beads become an indication of wealth.

A Quichua grandmother. The headdress is typical for older women.

Mama Manuela and her husband, Taita Antolino.

Evelyn, with a tapestry woven by the Incas, an embroidered blouse done by the Imbabura Indians, the Quichua New Testament and figures of a Quichua couple.

Dolores Morales, Evelyn's special co-worker in Agato. She was like a sister to Evelyn.

Evelyn checking an ear in the clinic. Her practical nursing came in handy.

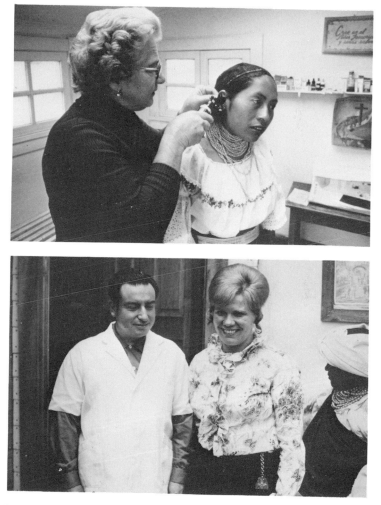

Marge and Marcelo Endara.

Evelyn, with Dolores, singing at the Silent Market, a weekly event in Otavalo.

The Alliance Evangelical Church in Agato on its dedication day, March 29, 1991. Note the logo in the window.

The new Spanish church in Otavalo. Evelyn had a significant influence in the beginnings of this church.

Baptismal service at Lake San Pablo.

The training center in Otavalo.

10

The Silent Market

The Indian market held on Saturday mornings in Otavalo was so famous in South America that busloads of gawking tourists arrived from Quito almost every week to see the spectacle. The Hotel Quito packed lunches for their guests who wanted to visit the market. It would be quite inadvisable for people from other countries to eat the variety of local foods offered there.

Many tourists arrived on Friday afternoon with instructions to retire early in preparation for rising at the crack of dawn. After a continental breakfast at the Hotel Otavalo, they would walk the five blocks to the market. Even at that early hour, most of the best ponchos were already sold. Only the Indians would know that. What was left was still very beautiful and attractive to souvenir-gathering people from all over the world.

Gorgeous woven blazers, tapestries, blankets, scarves, ponchos, embroidered dresses and blouses, leather goods and carved wooden figurines were all sold at unbelievably low prices.

All 27 guest rooms at Marge and Marcelo's

Hotel Otavalo were usually filled with tourists on Friday night. It was the only place in town where meals could be found that were safe for the tourists' stomachs and the beds compared favorably with the ones back home. Indian believers hired by Marge served as maids and bell boys. The Otavalan waitresses adorned themselves with layer upon layer of gold beads pressing heavily against exquisitely hand-embroidered, white cotton blouses. Their colorful costumes helped to create an atmosphere that was a tourist's delight.

On the market day itself activity began even before the roosters had stretched their necks to announce the dawn. While the guests still slept and long before dawn replaced the icy blasts of wind with the long golden rays of the sun on well-worn trails, the Indians were en route to the market. Slipping silently down the slopes of Taita Imbabura and the other jagged peaks that rimmed the world around Otavalo, their bare feet made scarcely a sound on the powder-dirt of the ancient trails. The unbelievably heavy load on each back was staggering to look at, let alone to carry. Often it was two or three times as large as the Indian to whom it was securely strapped. Beneath the stars, human trickles merged into human rivulets, then into human streams, which finally formed human rivers in the cobblestone streets of Otavalo.

For the hard-working Indian, day had arrived long before night had fled. And for Evelyn? At

4:30 a.m. a light blinked on feebly in one of the tall windows of the Spanish-style Hotel Otavalo. It was in Evelyn's apartment. Marcelo and Marge had invited her to use two rooms for a personal apartment. Evelyn had fixed it up beautifully. In exchange for its use, she helped manage the hotel when her services were needed.

Long before the excited tourists would hear the soft knock of an Indian on their door, Evelyn had readied herself both physically and spiritually for one of her busiest days of the week. There were boxes of books, Bibles, tracts, flannelgraph materials, etc., to be loaded in the Blazer. She could not do this the day before, though she would have preferred to. The threat of theft was too great. It was never wise to leave anything in your vehicle, not even in your own garage.

Evelyn's ministry of music, book-selling and tract distribution at the market would not begin until well after daybreak, but she knew that if she did not get down there early she would lose the parking spot at the edge of the market where the Indians were now accustomed to expecting her. The Indians knew where everything was supposed to be in the market. The layout seldom deviated even one foot. Only the gringos, unaware of the prescribed order, wandered about aimlessly in the well-arranged rows. The Indians were sure that the gringos had money, but certainly not brains. In fact, the very word "gringo" was sometimes served up with a generous supply of contempt.

Another name for the market was the Silent Market. Visitors found it amazing that 3,000 or more Indians could mill around with hardly a discernible sound. This enabled Evelyn's music, played over a sound system, to be clearly heard without having it blaring.

By eight o'clock in the morning, when most of the Indians had completed their purchases, they would start to pay more attention to Evelyn's tailgate bookstore. How she wished she could feel that the people were the hungry-hearted and not just the curious! Perhaps some of them were. If not, well, God could use curiosity, too.

Evelyn was encouraged that month by month, year in and year out, the sales of Christian literature and Bibles were on the increase. There was no breakthrough in the number of converts that she could call phenomenal, but the distribution of Christian literature and Bibles certainly was an encouragement. God had said that His Word would always produce fruit and accomplish all that He planned. Evelyn clung to that promise.

Stifling a yawn born not of boredom but of early rising, Evelyn thanked the Lord for the curious who stopped to listen as she presented the gospel with the aid of her flannelgraph. *Someday this powerful gospel will break through into hundreds and even thousands of lives, deliver-*

ing them from their spiritual wretchedness, she kept telling herself. Yes. A breakthrough. A breakthrough was what they needed. Was that too much to expect?

Surely God cared about these inhabitants of Imbabura, didn't He?

Evelyn had to believe that the heart for Imbabura He had given to her was but a miniature of His own great heart of love.

Do God's promises lose their lustre when years of dedicated labor produce next to nothing? The roster of missionary names with time/life/energy investments in Agato was growing longer with every year that passed. The roster of the thoroughly converted was not.

Evelyn plodded on, waiting for the breakthrough.

11

Come Over and Help Us

Jose Bonilla and Jose Cabascango sat on the long bench beside the Mission house and listened to Mama Manuela tell the gospel story as they awaited their turn to see the nurse. Taita Bonilla needed medical attention, but the men had another purpose in coming to Agato that day.

"In Morochos, where we live, there is an abandoned chapel," Jose Cabascango informed Evelyn. "Taita Bonilla owns it. We would like you to come to hold services in it."

Evelyn was excited to hear the news, but life was so packed with other things to do and people to reach that she did not find time to visit Morochos.

Months passed. Then, one day, the owner of the chapel reappeared at Evelyn's door. Again, Taita Bonilla pled for someone to come and hold services in Morochos. Responding to the importunity of the visitor, Evelyn arranged for Mama Manuela to go along with her and Azucena Ramirez, her Ecuadorian colleague.

The day of the planned expedition arrived. Mama Manuela would be in charge of leading them to Morochos. She knew the way, she said.

Everything went well until they reached Cotacachi. There they turned off the main road. Even Evelyn knew the way that far. Soon the road deteriorated into a wide trail and then a narrower trail. Finally, Mama Manuela admitted she was lost. She had come there by foot before, but never in a car. Everything, she said, looked different from the higher vantage point.

The women decided that they should stop to inquire. Bringing the Blazer to a halt on the dusty road, Evelyn approached an Indian. Before she could speak, however, he asked, "Have you heard that the body of Christ is being taken from house to house in this area? Would you like to see the body?"

"Oh, yes!" Evelyn replied. She found the prospect of seeing the "body of Christ" most interesting.

The man led them to a mud house where the patio was elaborately decorated with flowers.

"It is in this house," he said, pointing to the door.

As the women approached, another Indian stepped directly in front of them and blew a number of loud blasts on a conch shell. Chills ran up and down Evelyn's spine. She was in enemy territory and she knew it. *Could the blasts possibly be summoning people for an uprising?* she wondered.

The Indian guide sensed their nervousness.

"This is not for bad, but for good," he said. "They are announcing that the body is about to be moved to a different house and they are calling the faithful to accompany it."

The women entered the house. The mud walls of the interior were draped with white sheets. The room was set up like a chapel. On a table sat an elaborately carved wooden box, the size of a casket. Candles were burning in front of it. Inside was the "body of Christ" (probably a wax figure), complete with nail prints and bruised head. As each Indian filed past the coffin, he kissed the feet, side, hands and head.

Dear, sweet, godly, fearless Mama Manuela, sensing the spiritual darkness and deception, knelt on the floor and began to pray aloud, pleading with God to help these people come to know the living Christ. Evelyn did nothing, remembering that this was indeed hostile turf.

Another blast of the conch shell. With much ceremony the body was lifted and carried by six men to another house. Children scattered flowers in the path. The villagers, plus Evelyn and Mama Manuela, walked behind. Each house would have the privilege of hosting the body for a fee of five sucres per day, payable to the church.

The three women finally arrived in Morochos hours later. Taita Cabascango, Mama Manuela's half-brother, welcomed them warmly. Soon, a small crowd, including Taita Bonilla, arrived at the crude Cabascango hut-home. Evelyn held a brief service.

The main purpose for the visit, however, was to see the chapel that held the possibility of becoming a lighthouse in Morochos. As the believers marched single file up the trail to the abandoned chapel, Evelyn was reminded of the procession earlier in the day. But this time it was different. A living Christ was being carried, not in a box, but in the hearts and bodies of these believers. This living Christ was about to establish a living Church right there in Satan's territory.

Before leaving Morochos, Evelyn and Azucena visited several homes and had prayer with each family. Yes, there was at least a nucleus of interested people here at Morochos.

Week after week Evelyn returned to Morochos with medicines and the gospel. The chapel they thought was owned by Taita Bonilla turned out to be a community chapel. It wasn't long until the government, perhaps in an effort to repel the spread of the gospel in that area, sent a nurse to live there and serve the people. Another house of worship would have to be found.

"Let's build our own chapel," some of the believers suggested. It was an idea that proved to be supported by both enthusiasm and determination. One believer provided a piece of

land. Work bees were arranged. Frames were
constructed and roped together. Dirt was tossed
inside the walls. Water was added to make it
moist. The men then trampled down the moist
earth with their feet and pounded it down with
huge mallets. The mud walls began to go up.
With the mud thoroughly dried and the frames
taken away, the walls looked almost like cement.
Here in Morochos, there was now a sanctuary
that would glorify God, the living God.

Another outpost for the gospel had been
established in Imbabura—and the gates of hell
would not be able to prevail against it.

12

Teniente to the Rescue

A teacher from the St. Paul Bible College accompanied a group of students to Ecuador to see Mission work first hand. Evelyn welcomed them warmly. Her rhubarb pie was delicious. Even those who were sure they did not like rhubarb pie were in for a surprise. It was sweet! Well, at least not terribly tart as most rhubarb pies are.

"Tomorrow morning," Evelyn announced to the enthusiastic group, "I am going to take you to Morochos. God has begun a work among the people of that area. You will be blessed to see it and they will be blessed by your coming. Bring your instruments along and we will hold a service there."

By breakfast time at the Hotel Otavalo, Evelyn had already loaded the Land Rover with her accordion, flannelgraph board (the people always loved to have her "talk with pictures"), her little black satchel filled with medicines for the sick and lots of tracts.

"As we ride along you may throw tracts out the windows whenever we pass Indians," she suggested.

The students couldn't get over the way the people scrambled for the tracts and often immediately sat down by the side of the road to read them, or ran home to find someone who could read it to them.

As Evelyn entered a narrow-streeted town with a string of packed mud buildings at street's edge on either side, she shouted above the noise of the Land Rover: "This is Quiroga. The people of Quiroga are quite antagonistic to the gospel. About 10 years ago Gordon Loptson and Señor Cabascango passed through here to visit a new believer on up the road. On their return, 200 people attacked them with mud, dirt, stones, clubs and burning rags. Señor Cabascango received a hard blow to the back of his head. Gordon had a gash on his cheek and his glasses were broken. Both had many stone bruises on their legs and backs. Some simpatizantes (sympathizers) with the gospel finally rescued them from the angry mob."

Even as Evelyn spoke, a clod of dirt smashed against the Land Rover. Evelyn thought about the many times she had driven up here alone and thanked the Lord for His faithful protection. Several times Indians signaled for Evelyn and the group to stop. One asked for medicine to cure deformity. Another wanted diarrhea pills. Yet another asked for a pill for sadness. Finally, the vehicle headed out of town.

With little warning the road ended. As Evelyn bounced the Land Rover down into the riverbed, the students and their professor grabbed for whatever was handy. The rocky channel made the vehicle seem like a fragile toy in danger of disintegration. As for Evelyn, she just gripped the wheel tighter and leaned forward. It was a relief to everyone when they finally pulled back out of the stony bed. A short distance ahead the vehicle humped and bumped once more, this time over the plough ridges of a cornfield. Finally breaking out into a clearing, Evelyn pointed with pride at the four walls of packed mud representing the sacrificial beginnings of the church building in Morochos.

The Indians had already gathered in the nearby thatched-roof hut. Their singing was heavenly, its sound surpassed only by the joyful expressions which counter-balanced the poverty of their surroundings. *They are rich*, Evelyn thought, *rich with the riches of God in Christ Jesus.*

Two of the students played a trombone duet they had worked up especially for the trip. The people loved it. Before the service was over, they had played it three times!

Evelyn sat on the floor playing her accordion. Next to her perched a very dirty little Indian girl with an adorable, round face and black, sparkling eyes. And on the other side of the girl sat one of the college students. Because the student came from a wealthy family, the professor had not been at all sure how she would react to the squalor of the villages. Could she, who had enjoyed everything that money could buy, adapt herself to the poverty of rural Ecuador? Would she be able to sit, as they were now being asked to do, on the dirt floor of an Indian home?

Evelyn watched with interest out of the corner of her eye as the round-faced little girl with golden beads layered around her neck looked up at the student and smiled a very dirty, but a very sweet little smile.

Suddenly, the student reached out, put her arm around the little girl and drew her in close. The professor's eyes filled with tears. What he was seeing was love in a language that could be understood.

After the service, Concepción, one of the Indian women, asked Evelyn to come to her nearby hut. The visiting professor and a couple of the students joined her. Concepción's elderly mother was extremely ill.

The group ducked their heads as they filed through the under-sized opening in the wall of the hut. It took a moment or two for their eyes to adjust to the windowless darkness. Cui (pronounced kwee; guinea pigs) scurried along by the wall, their beady red eyes reflecting the meager shaft of light from the doorway. On a mat in the corner, the mother sat cross-legged— a wrinkly-skinned, shriveled, old woman, rocking back and forth and moaning softly.

Evelyn explained to the visitors, "Concepción wants me to try once again to get her mother to understand the way of salvation, but her mother is deaf, perhaps totally deaf. She wants me to shout the gospel to her."

It was an unforgettable scene. Evelyn knelt directly in front of the dying woman. She put one hand on each of her bony shoulders and, aiming her voice toward one ear, shouted the plan of salvation in the Quichua language into ears that could not hear. The professor turned and, facing the mud wall, sobbed quietly.

The old woman died without Christ. For Concepción's mother, the gospel came too late. If only their area had opened earlier. . . . But there was no time for lamenting the past. There were the living to reach. Some areas, like Morochos, were beginning to open to the gospel now, and Evelyn determined that she would give all her strength to reaching the people of Imbabura. The burden of her heart was a burden for Imbabura.

The little group in Morochos continued to grow, but so did the opposition. Religious leaders threatened excommunication from the community itself if these evangelicals persisted in building their chapel. The mud walls they were erecting would be torn down, they said.

A representative of the established church came by to collect tithes from the community members: a row of corn for every 10 rows they had planted. The believers refused to pay, stating boldly that their tithes would go to God and not to the priest or to the church. Their refusal prompted additional threats about destroying the evangelical chapel.

Early one morning a knock came at Evelyn's door in Agato. It was Manuel Jeres from Morochos. He was weeping!

"Señorita Evelina," he cried, "come quickly, please! People from three communities are coming to break down the walls of our chapel."

Evelyn was advised not to go to Morochos alone. Perhaps a police escort would be the answer. The police claimed that the matter was out of their jurisdiction.

"But," they said, "there is a teniente who happens to be in town who has jurisdiction everywhere. He won't be at the office until eight o'clock, however."

Evelyn decided to ask a local believer to accompany her. As they were about to leave Otavalo, the teniente approached. He was dressed in a military-style uniform and looked most impressive, striding like a soldier and bristling with self-importance. Evelyn was encouraged. The police officer's suggestion had been a good one. Just how good Evelyn was about to find out!

Evelyn explained the problem at Morochos to the teniente and he agreed to go with her. He took along canisters of tear gas and several soldiers with rifles. Evelyn's Land Rover was quite a sight as it finally pulled out of Otavalo. There was Taita Jeres, the believer from Morochos, the teniente, four armed soldiers and Evelyn as the chauffeur.

As they passed through Quiroga, Evelyn told the teniente how the people there often spat at her and threw mud when she passed through. It was nice to have him along this time. No mud was thrown at them.

"We will take care of that situation on the way back," the teniente said firmly.

When Evelyn pulled into the clearing at Morochos, everything was quiet. There was no sign of any disturbance and no people in sight. *Oh, what if this was all simply propaganda!* she thought. She would surely feel foolish if that were the case. But as the car stopped, some believers rushed toward the vehicle.

"They are all over there," they pointed, "in the bushes by the community church."

It was true. Fifty men armed with machetes were waiting for one more group to arrive before attempting to tear down the chapel the evangelicals had nearly finished. A sense of relief swept over Evelyn as the teniente took charge.

Striding boldy in the direction of the potential aggressors, he demanded,

"What are you doing here?"

"Oh, nothing," they replied, "we just came for a minga (work bee)."

"Where is the minga?" the teniente asked.

There was none.

The teniente tried to find out who the leader

of the group was. No one would tell. He then made the men come one by one and lay down their machetes in front of him. After additional probing, they finally acknowledged that the religious leaders in Quiroga had urged them to defend their faith by demolishing the soon-to-be-completed church.

"We don't want these evangelicals here," they said. "We are of another faith."

"So am I," responded the teniente, "but in Ecuador we have religious liberty, and they have as much right to worship as we do."

"But we don't want them in this community," the group insisted.

"Unless they tie you up with ropes and carry you into their chapel and make you listen, you have no right to hack down their walls. If I hear of any more disturbances of this kind, the leaders of your communities will be the first to be put in jail."

Then addressing himself to Evelyn, he asked, "Do you want me to lock them all up?"

"No," Evelyn replied. "We want to work with these people."

After more lecturing, the teniente picked up one of the machetes.

"Whose machete is this?" he demanded.

A man came forward.

"Take it, and go home. Now! Alone!"

The teniente picked up another and did the same thing until all the machetes were gone.

On the way home to Agato, Evelyn stopped

the vehicle in Quiroga. The teniente gathered the village hecklers together and gave them a lecture similar to the one he had delivered earlier in Morochos.

It worked. The people of Quiroga never again threw mud at Evelyn. They just glared at her every time she drove through their village.

13

Too Close for Comfort

Taita (Father) Rafael was working in the kitchen of the old stuccoed Mission house. Skillfully wielding a huge knife, he patiently diced the onions he had just pulled from the compound garden. His big, motherly apron and his shiny black hair pulled back into a long braid belied the respectful title "Taita Rafael." Except for his obviously masculine build atop those short legs, he looked more like a matronly maid than the hired hand that he was.

Taita Rafael had been sober for quite a few weeks now. That was a praise-producing victory. Some of the Otavalan Indians were instantly delivered from their drinking when they became Christians, but Taita Rafael had not found instantaneous victory. In spite of that, it was an undeniable fact that his love for the Lord was deep and real.

Jerry and Carol Conn chatted with Evelyn in the combination living room/dining area as they huddled near the big stone fireplace that cut across one corner of the room. No one took the time to analyze why they always sat so near the fire. Perhaps it was because of the almost perpetual morning chill at 9,300 feet in the Andes.

It's a wonder anyone heard the soft knock at the kitchen door. Taita Rafael certainly didn't. He had no hearing aid and his hearing loss had long since blocked out most knocks, particularly the feather-soft Quichua knocks.

"Taita Rafael!" Evelyn yelled out, unhappy with the raucous sound of her voice. She hated yelling. Her own soft-spoken manner made her naturally well-adapted to this quiet, Quichua culture.

"Taita Rafael!" she called again, reluctantly raising her voice a few more decibels. "See if there is someone at the door."

Taita Rafael laid down the machete/knife, wiped an onion-induced tear from his eye and shuffle-walked toward the door.

There stood Enma Salvador, a sister in Christ. Her bold witness and honest burden for her relatives were well known and respected among fellow evangelicals.

"Buenos días, señora," the old Indian said with a warm smile.

"Buenos días, Taita. Cómo está? (How are you?)" she countered.

"Muy bien, gracias (Very well, thank you)," he answered, following the customary progression and totally ignoring the fact that his arthritis made his answer a lie.

Traditional greetings out of the way, Enma

asked to see the Conns and Evelyn. She knew Evelyn was there. Her mud-splattered Land Rover was parked in the compound driveway. Jerry and Carol Conn were the missionaries currently living on the station. Evelyn lived down in Otavalo, sharing an apartment with her colleagues, Vi Wangen and Azucena Ramirez.

Evelyn rose to welcome Enma with a traditional abrazo (embrace). "Buenos días, mi hermana! (Good morning, my sister)."

Following a vigorous round of handshakes with everyone in the room, Enma quickly got down to the reason for her visit.

"My brother-in-law, Señor Erazo, has sent me a message from Selva Alegre. You know how isolated that little group of believers is. They would like to have another visit from the missionaries and me as soon as possible. Could you plan a trip with me pronto to strengthen these brothers and sisters in the Lord?

"Also, Señor Portilla, one of my relatives, would like to be married to the woman he is living with. He wants people to be reminded that believers can be married in the evangelical church, proving that they have the same rights as the Catholics. They would like you to have children's meetings, too, and there are others who want to be baptized. Will you come?"

Evelyn winced as she recalled a former trip to Selva Alegre. She remembered how Jerry Conn had complained for days about his "pants hurting him" after those five hours of riding on a horse that was so short-legged that Jerry's feet almost dragged on the ground. Evelyn's own horse had been almost impossible, too. In fact, she would say "impossible" was indeed the correct word. Evelyn had been forced to abandon the horse when he refused to do anything she wanted. Enma, who had ridden her own beautiful riding horse, had graciously exchanged it for Evelyn's incorrigible beast. It was like exchanging a Cadillac for a Jeep.

Azucena, the petite graduate of the Seminario in Guayaquil, had been along on that trip also. She had never ridden a horse in her life. Fear had stimulated her muscles, tensing them into painful cramps. Every part of her body ached. The sisters in Selva Alegre had daubed her body from head to toe with hot mud to ease her agony.

But what a beautiful, warm reception the people had given them as they arrived. Jerry had performed a wedding. Some babies had been dedicated. Evelyn had conducted children's meetings using flannelgraph lessons. How the people had loved the singing! In the evening evangelistic meetings had been held. The little group of evangelicals were strong, not in number, but in spirit and in their walk with the Lord.

The townspeople too, although almost entirely non-evangelical, had been politely friendly, half-smiling as the strange-looking foreigners had passed the doorways of their mud houses. Not often did they see a gringo in this remote mountain village. Selva Alegre was no tourist stop.

The arrival of these unusual, light-haired, blue-eyed, fair-skinned people had been an interesting and welcome event for all except a few. The religious opposition had been caught off guard. They had not had time to stir up the people against the missionaries. So, all in all, it had been a good visit. God had accomplished His purposes.

Evelyn's thoughts jerked back from her reveries as Taita Rafael dropped another log on the fire causing spitting, firecracker-like objections. Jerry was answering Enma Salvador in his unique, slowly-enunciated Spanish.

Jerry assured Enma that they would be most willing to try to arrange for another trip to her relatives and to the Selva Alegre believers. He and Carol, however, would not be able to go. They were due for furlough. Perhaps Evelyn and Vi could make the trip.

A tentative date was arranged for the second missionary journey to Selva Alegre. Evelyn purposed that, with God's help, they would strengthen the tiny, sincere, but isolated, band of believers.

The day of their departure dawned clearer than usual. Even Taita Imbabura had shyly pulled away his veil of clouds and revealed his towering head. It was lightly dusted with snow, as if his hair were white—sparse, but beautiful. The heart on his massive slopes was so clearly visible that one could almost imagine it beating.

The little group of travelers that gathered in Otavalo didn't see the brief shower up against the mountain that occasioned a rainbow. But the Indians who caught a glimpse of the rainbow sensed an instinctive dread of the day that lay before them. Who could tell what evil the diabolical author of that rainbow intended by revealing himself like that? Everyone knew the meaning of the rainbow—it was a symbol of the diablo himself.

For Evelyn and her traveling companions (Vi Wangen, Enma Salvador, Enrique Varela, Polivio Erazo and Victor Tohala, the pastor) that glimpse of the rainbow would have been a wonderful memory to carry with them over treacherous trails into danger and the threat of death. But they had not seen the rainbow. Neither did they know of the dangers they would face that day. The first was a pity, for the beauty of the rainbow had escaped them. The second was a mercy, for God in love often throws a veil across our way.

Their only dread as they waited for the bus that would take them to Apuela was of the trail that lay before them—oh yes, and of the kind of horse that might become their lot among the motley crew of beasts of burden that would be assembled.

The Apuela bus pulled up to the curb in

Otavalo and disgorged its incoming passengers. The baggage of the waiting travelers was then tossed up to the man on top of the bus. He secured it all in the luggage rack, piling it so high that it made the bus look dangerously top-heavy. Evelyn and crew climbed aboard the rickety bus.

They waited and waited. The bus didn't move. Evelyn noticed that the streets in front of the bus were gridlocked by assorted traffic. Since going forward seemed impossible, the driver decided to back out. A young "conductor" shouted from the back of the bus, "Okay! Okay! Okay!" The "stop!" came too late. There was a loud thud. Fortunately, the damages turned out to be minor and, after much motioning and hollering, the bus started on its way.

The aging vehicle groaned ominously as it pulled up out of the Otavalo basin and started snaking over the Pan American Highway toward Apuela and the Colombian border. Evelyn thought about the difference between what that highway was really like and the mental images "Pan American Highway" would conjure up in the minds of friends back home. This narrow, cobblestone road snaked for miles through rugged mountain terrain, detouring deeply into each ravine before crossing a narrow bridge and climbing back out of the creek bed. The countless hairpin-like executions were a real endurance test. The top-heavy truck/bus churned up great clouds of dust as it careened around curve after curve. Three hours' worth of curves later it reached Apuela.

Evelyn was so thankful that motion sickness had never been a problem for her. How much easier it would have been to have come in the Land Rover, but there was no place to leave it in Apuela while they were in the interior. It would certainly have been stolen.

In Apuela, the group clustered around a hole-in-the-wall restaurant. Some bought sopa de pollo (chicken soup). Others purchased cui (guinea pig). If one could get past their resemblance to roasted rats, it would be possible to enjoy the taste. The cui were roasted whole to a golden brown and delicately spiced. The head was considered the choice piece. Evelyn preferred the hind legs. They had more meat on them. A plate of cooked rice with a fried egg on top and some lentils completed the repast and guaranteed freedom from hunger pains along the trail. One never knew what other types of problems might inconveniently develop, however, after eating in an Apuela restaurant.

The pack horses were already arriving as the group finished eating. They had made the three-hour trek out from Selva Alegre early that morning laden with raspadura (brown sugar bars) and other such marketable products to sell in Apuela. Now they would carry their human loads back into the isolated village during the early afternoon hours.

The men helped load the horses with bundles of personal clothing, used Christmas cards (for awards), children's meeting materials, a guitar, flannelgraph lessons, accordion, the black satchel filled with medicines for the sick, bathroom tissue (a must for every trip) and some foods that were not obtainable in the interior.

Enma was to be the guide for the women who would go on ahead. The men had a long list of supplies to obtain before they could leave for Selva Alegre.

Evelyn never had become so accustomed to the beauty of these Andes that she could take it all in stride without spontaneously worshipping the One Who had made this lofty mountain grandeur. Were there really any mountains more impressive in all the world? She was sure that not even the rugged, towering Himalayas could be any more beautiful than these of her beloved Imbabura.

Taita Imbabura and its relatives shone particularly green and luxurious this morning. Two-thirds of the way up their slopes they were wrapped in the most beautiful patchwork quilts. The fenced-in gardens of the industrious, high-mountain Quichua looked for all the world like carefully handcrafted quilts in blending shades of yellow, green, ochre and brown. Eucalyptus groves—tall, green and stately—were enclosed by giant cabuya cactus with bluish-green spears leaping fountain-like from the center in every direction.

For Vi Wangen it was the first trip to the interior. For Evelyn, the second. Evelyn observed facetiously with her characteristic good-natured chuckle and a twinkle in her eye that she didn't know which was worse—the fear of the unknown that plagued Vi, or the memory of the known that plagued her.

The trail was extremely muddy this time. The passing of many cargo horses had formed deep holes where each hoof had been placed. Now the horses seemed to choose those very holes to fill with their own hoofs. The exaggerated plop! plop! plop! reminded Evelyn of the "Donkey Serenade."

The first challenge—crossing the swinging bridge—proved to be quite a frightening experience. The horses went one at a time. More than one horse with its cargo would have been too much weight for the flimsy, swaying bridge to handle.

The sight of a large rock up the valley triggered an instant replay of the last time Evelyn had passed this way. With a spontaneous shudder, she prayed that God would get them all safely past. She needed no medical apparatus to verify her rising blood pressure and accelerating heartbeat. This would be her third reluctant pass around that rock perched high on the side of the ravine. *There are some things,* she thought whimsically, *that do not become easier with practice.* Evelyn decided that there was only one thing to do—give the horse some slack, hold on tightly to the saddle and close her eyes.

She could feel the horse edging along the precipitous trail. It seemed like an eternity was passing as she held on, eyes closed, to the reins. Supposing that by this time the horse must be around the Gibraltar-like rock, Evelyn opened her eyes for a peek. If only she had looked to the right toward the rock instead of to the left, it would have been so much better.

No path was visible! Only hundreds of feet of vertical wall.

With an involuntary gasp she closed her eyes more tightly than ever and dug her fingernails even deeper into the saddle.

The next half-opening of her eyes signaled her brain the right to breathe again, and, along with the breath of rarefied air, she breathed an earnest prayer of thanksgiving to the One Who had promised that He would give His angels charge over her, lest she should dash her foot against a stone. Apparently that promise extended to her horse's hooves as well!

Two men came into view as the three women rounded a bend on the trail. One was dressed in clerical garb. That was not normally a disturbing sight. But these two men were not moving. Instead, they were waiting, blocking the narrow trail with their bodies and their horses.

The priest was a Jesuit, complete with clerical robes and a little black felt hat. His companion was a burly-looking fellow, huge and towering, dressed in work clothes. The women approached apprehensively.

"You cannot come in here," the priest advised sternly as the women came within earshot. "You are not welcome. The people do not want you. You are not welcome!"

Evelyn turned to Vi and Enma.

"What shall we do? Where shall we go?" she asked in whispered tones.

It was Enma who responded. With fire in her eyes, she almost shouted, "We go right ahead, that's what we do!" Enma was not one to be easily intimidated, either by the priest or his henchman.

Turning directly toward the men, Enma continued, "I have relatives in Selva Alegre. They have invited us to come. We intend to visit them. We have every right to go in there. We are going in!"

The priest glared at Enma.

"Then I am not responsible for what happens to you. You are not wanted. The people are upset that you are coming. I cannot be responsible for your safety."

Enma glared right back. She knew the man. She knew his reputation.

"The way you live and the evil things you do are no secret," Enma insisted. "We know what you are like. You command no respect, even among the people of your parish. You are religious, but you are not righteous."

The anger in the priest's flushed face was

evident. He had no defense. What Enma was saying was the truth and he knew it.

Evelyn remained silent, quietly observing the confrontation. She would not have dared to speak in such a fashion.

Enma plunged ahead.

"Why are the people agitated?" she demanded. "Is it because you have incited trouble?"

There was no response.

Without a further word, Enma picked up the reins of her horse and pressed it forward past the priest and his silent, but menacing morale booster. Evelyn and Vi followed. In some ways, the threats of this priest and the silence of his bodyguard struck more fear in Evelyn than the clods of earth that had been thrown each time she had passed through Quiroga. Were they the precursors of things to come?

The men whirled their horses, galloped past the women, splashed through the river and disappeared around a bend in the trail. Evelyn could not forget the look in the eyes of the priest nor the tone of his voice. She knew how the priests hated the evangelicals. Word had spread about the massive inroads of the "heretics" in other areas such as Salasaca and the Oriente. These people wanted no such inroads of the gospel into their territory.

A rise in the trail was followed immediately by an abrupt drop into a basin-like area. Cresting the little hill, Evelyn was startled to see a large crowd of peasants gathered below. Apart from the Silent Market on Saturday mornings down in Otavalo she had never seen a crowd like this on a non-festival day.

In the midst of the crowd the priest and his muscular side-kick huddled together with others in clerical robes. Off to one side stood a donkey with a big piece of tin tied platform-like on top of it. Beside the donkey lay a huge pile of bamboo. A terrifying thought pierced both Evelyn and Vi simultaneously: *Could it be that that is a platform on which they will burn us alive?* It was a frightful prospect.

Oh, where are the men? Evelyn half-wondered, half-prayed. *If only they would come!*

14

Angels in Charge

Speak up!" Enma demanded as the priests tried to hush their conversation. "Speak up so everyone can hear you!"

Meanwhile, at the end of the valley, the rest of Evelyn's party crested the hill. Seeing the crowd gathered below, the men knew instinctively that something was wrong. They spurred their horses into a full gallop and headed toward the crowd. The women breathed a prayer of thanksgiving. Briefly, they reviewed the happenings on the trail and the predicament of the moment.

Mr. Erazo stepped forward to lead the discussion. As the teniente político in Selva Alegre, he had the authority that was needed for this situation.

"Religious liberty is guaranteed by our constitution," he reminded the crowd. "You have no right to prohibit us from entering this area!"

The priest countered. "We have heard that you are coming in to tear down the Catholic church and replace it with an evangelical one. All these people have come to prevent your entry. They do not want you in here. Your group must go back."

"It is not true that we plan to tear down the Catholic church," Mr. Erazo insisted. "We do plan to build an evangelical church, yes! But that is my project. It will not interfere with your right to worship."

For nearly an hour the arguing continued. Some of the crowd fingered their machetes and guns.

Again the priest insisted, "You may not go in! At least your friends may not go in with you."

"My friends will go in with me," the teniente responded with even more authority in his voice. Then, turning to Evelyn, he ordered, "Señorita Evelina, move ahead."

Evelyn tried to press her horse forward but someone grabbed the reins and held her back. Mr. Erazo continued to argue with the priests.

Suddenly a spokesman from the crowd said, "All right, go ahead, then, but you are not to visit in the homes of the people in Selva Alegre, nor may you propagate your gospel."

Now the crowd was really angry, but not with Mr. Erazo and the missionaries. They were angry with the priests.

"They [the priests] took us out of our fields and brought us all this distance. We have had nothing to eat all day. We came to stop the heretics from coming in. Now they are letting them go."

More shouting and arguing followed. Finally, both groups dispersed, each going its own way.

Evelyn and her entourage spent another tense
hour on the trail, ascending and descending
precipitously, and then climbing to what seemed
like the very top of the world. Selva Alegre
was built on a high plateau at the very crest of
the mountain.

As they approached a bridge near the
entrance to the town, two believers met them.

"Please wait here for the rest of the believers,"
they said. "The people of the town are hostile.
They may try to stop us. We must all go in
together."

Once again, Mr. Erazo took the lead. This
time there were no friendly faces in the doorways. Only angry glares.

Mrs. Erazo was waiting for them at home.
How refreshing the glass of cold naranjilla juice
tasted! Dinner was also ready—chicken soup
and arroz con pollo, a delectable dish of rice
and chicken. Mrs. Erazo had known about the
tensions and the crowd that had gone to stop
them. She had spent many anxious hours awaiting their arrival. Now, it was a relief to be able
to busy herself with setting food on the table for
the long-awaited guests.

It would probably be wise, the group decided
as they ate, to have no gathering of the evangelical congregation that evening even though it
was scheduled for this large, impressive home of
the teniente himself.

"Let the anger subside," someone suggested.
They all agreed. Darkness settled like a blanket

over the hamlet.

No sooner had the sun hidden its face than the church bell in the center of town began to ring. It was the signal for the faithful to gather in the big church in the square. Evelyn, Vi, Enma, the Erazo family and Pastor Tohala went upstairs for a prayer meeting. They didn't know what the people were hearing in the church nearby, but they could imagine. And sometimes imaginations are more terrifying than reality. Their fears, it turned out, were not unfounded.

Soon an angry crowd flowed out of the church and began to surround the Erazo home. Clods of dirt slammed against the walls.

"Long live the Catholic religion!" they shouted.

Señor Erazo interrupted the prayer meeting. "I will go down and talk with the people," he volunteered. "I think they will listen to me. I am, after all, the teniente político of this village."

The rest of the group intensified their prayers as Mr. Erazo opened the front door. Clods of earth and stones pummelled the doorway as he did so. Shots blazed into the air. Torches twirled menacingly. Angry voices hurled insults. Señor Erazo slammed the door shut.

Meanwhile, upstairs, Pastor Tohala read to the terrified group: "He shall give His angels charge over you." "No evil shall befall you." The group continued to pray, claiming God's protection over them and over the house itself. Evelyn hoped that some of her supporters back home would also sense the burden to pray.

As the evening dragged on, one by one the mob slipped away and silence slowly settled over the Erazo household. Exhausted, each one retired for the night.

In the morning, government inspectors came to the door to report to the teniente that they had taken four men into custody the night before. They had been found operating a still.

One of the inspectors was the son-in-law of the governor of the province of Imbabura. Mr. Erazo, realizing that the timing was particularly appropriate, recounted the terrors of the night before. A telegram was sent to the governor implicating the priests as the instigators of the violence and asking for six policemen to come in to control the situation.

Evelyn and the others did not cut their visit short, but discreetly kept their gatherings low key. They did not wish to deliberately antagonize the opposition. It was later revealed that a story had been circulated by the priests that the people had risen up against the evangelicals and that it was the priests who had protected the endangered evangelicals!

No territory in Imbabura seemed to be claimed easily. Just as jealously as the Indians guarded their land holdings, so the enemy was challenging every inch of spiritual ground. Evelyn and her colleagues were not fighting against flesh and blood, but against principalities and powers and rulers of darkness.

For now, it seemed that the enemy was snatching away the seed as fast as it was being sown. But, God was on His throne. One day, the heart of Imbabura would rejoice!

The breakthrough would come.

15

Atuntaqui

S eñorita," the new believer from Atuntaqui (Ah-toon-ta'-kee) said politely, "we are only a few believers and we need encouragement. Would you come and teach us?"

Evelyn was, as always, glad to accept such an invitation, knowing full well that another battle in the heavenlies (and probably on earth besides) would ensue.

Atuntaqui proved to be no different from most of the other areas she had dared to enter. There was no gospel witness there and opposition was evident from the first day. It became even more obvious one day as Evelyn returned to her car after teaching a Vacation Bible School session. The vehicle had been plastered from bumper to bumper with manure.

"Leave, and never return to this area again," the milling crowd demanded, but Evelyn was not easily deterred. She returned the following day as usual.

One of her first stops in Atuntaqui was to pick up Señor Coralas' children. At the door, Evelyn was confronted by his angry, unbelieving wife.

"If you come back again to take my niños to those religious classes of yours," she threatened, "I will show you what I will do to you!" She went into the kitchen and promptly returned with a butcher knife.

Fortunately for all concerned, Señor Coralas walked into the room at that moment and insisted that the children go with Evelyn to the classes. Presenting the gospel in Atuntaqui was obviously an uphill battle all the way.

On Sunday, Evelyn decided to take a national pastor with her to help with the afternoon service. She also took several believers from Otavalo and San Antonio. As they were preparing to celebrate communion, an angry crowd approached. Once again the aggressors insisted that Evelyn and the others leave.

The believers spoke up. Did the group not remember that religious liberty was guaranteed in Ecuador? Did they not remember that the constitution allowed them to worship as they wished?

Sensing possible trouble, someone went for the police. But no police were to be found. The crowd continued to push and shove and threaten. They threw chunks of dirt. Unwilling to antagonize the villagers further, the Christians left.

A measure of apprehension now accompanied every trip to Atuntaqui as the believers continued to be persecuted. The villagers called the believers foreigners. They called them dogs.

They called them donkeys. They said that their
souls had been bought by the despised evangelicals. All of those statements were terrible
insults.

Something else added to the apprehension—
Evelyn could never be certain the police would
be there if trouble erupted. They could not be
counted on. But Evelyn was counting both on
God and the prayers of His people that she
and the local believers would be protected from
the onslaughts of enemies both seen and
unseen. Did the people back home know how
important their prayers were? Could they, did
they, understand that she and the others were
wrestling against principalities and powers and
rulers of darkness? Were they taking a stand on
her behalf against the onslaughts of Satan in the
province of Imbabura?

Evelyn thought of Dorothy and Effie
Postlethwaite. She had never met those dear
Canadian sisters, yet she knew they prayed for
her regularly and followed her every move.

She thought of Stanton and Hazel Richardson
back in St. Paul. She knew they, too, prayed for
her daily.

She thought about the many Women's
Missionary Prayer Fellowships that had committed themselves to prayer. Did they understand how crucial their prayers were to her
safety and to the persecuted group of despised
evangelicals in Imbabura Province?

She hoped that they did!

She desperately needed those prayers if the gospel was to gain a foothold, if the breakthrough was ever to come in darkened Imbabura.

16

If...

Evelyn blew out the light and crawled into bed. A strange feeling, not of fear, which would have been natural, but of comfort and peace flowed over her like a warm blanket. Living alone in the big, not-so-cozy Mission house, she could always summon help with the bell. It had saved her and Marge before. It could be counted on again. Just days later, however, the bell would not be where Evelyn needed it.

As Evelyn rounded the corner for the final stretch on the narrow, trail-like road leading to the Mission compound, she noticed a group of Indians blocking the road in front of the cantina (bar). In a gesture of friendship, she rolled down the car window as the Indians approached. But they were in no mood for friendship.

"Give us money to buy more liquor," they demanded, their words already slurred by too much to drink.

The aggressiveness of their demeanor propelled a sudden stab of fear to Evelyn's heart.

She noticed that clubs, stones and doubled-up fists were already supporting the crowd's demands. She decided to respond softly, gently. "Lord help me to get through this crowd!" Evelyn breathed her words as she pondered her reply.

"I am the missionary in this area," she reminded them. "We do not drink. We seek to please God in every way. I cannot give you money for liquor. It would be wrong for me to do it and it is wrong for you to drink." The crowd pressed closer.

It is now or never, Evelyn thought, her words falling on rebellious ears.

Slowly, deliberately, she shoved the Blazer into first gear and edged it forward, bodies against bumper, man against metal. Bloodshot eyes flashed hatred. Fists and clubs pummeled the vehicle. Evelyn tightened her grip on the steering wheel. With eyes locked on some point directly ahead, she pushed through the crowd and hurried on up the lonely road.

A sigh of relief and a prayer of thanksgiving escaped her lips as she finally turned into the Mission compound. It had been a close call, and so near home too. There had been too many close calls lately. Everyday seemed like a direct foray into battle—a battle that was both spiritual and now, increasingly physical. Another stab of fear shot unbeckoned through Evelyn's heart.

Where do I go from here? Should I stay in this

area when I know full well that the next time there could be very serious consequences? Could these incidents be God's way of saying that it is time to move on? The questions demanded an answer.

Evelyn poked the fire and curled up in the chair beside it. Moving her pressure lantern a little closer so she could read more easily, she picked up her New Testament. God's Word had always been her source of wisdom and guidance. Tonight would be no different.

She opened her Testament to Matthew chapter two.

"Be thou there until I bring thee word" leaped from the page. That was her answer. It was a message from God's heart to hers. It was all she needed. She would stay in Imbabura. God had told her to.

News of the frightening confrontation reached the field chairman, Henry Miller. This was no trivial matter. He decided that he would have to make a trip to the isolated Agato station to talk to Evelyn.

"I almost got into trouble for allowing you to come here alone in the first place," Henry Miller confessed as he and Evelyn sat in the living room. "And now I hear of this latest confrontation. I am concerned for you. The work has been hard here. There have been very few results. We have no one to assign to work with you here in Agato. The committee feels that you might like to work somewhere else, perhaps

Guayaquil where the Holy Spirit is moving. You could work at the Templo or at the Institute."

"And close down Agato? Pull out?" Evelyn was flabbergasted.

"Yes," Henry answered. "We feel it is just too hard a place for a single woman. And what's more, we've seen no significant manifestation of the working of the Lord in this area."

"Mr. Miller," Evelyn remonstrated as she straightened her shoulders, "if you can assure me that God is a respecter of persons and that He never plans to work among these people, I will move out tomorrow (Evelyn had just moved in the week before!), but I don't think anyone can assure me of that."

"No, it's not that," Henry Miller replied, somewhat taken aback. "It's just that the work is very, very difficult. Perhaps we should simply close up and go somewhere else."

Evelyn thought for a moment and then replied: "God has given me a verse saying that I am to stay here until He brings me word."

Evelyn's confident assurance caught Henry Miller by surprise. Who was he, as the field chairman, to argue with God or for that matter, with this determined woman?

Reluctantly, Mr. Miller decided that little remained for him to do except to commend Evelyn to God and allow her to continue her ministry to the heart of Imbabura.

"We don't know how you are going to do it, but if you want to stay, we will back you up in every way we can," he promised.

Matter closed.

Among the serendipities of life some four years earlier, Evelyn had received a letter and poem from Bert Sundberg, a member of her home church in Freedhem. How appropriate the poem seemed now, particularly the last two lines, in view of this turn of events at the Agato compound.

CONSIDER HIM—HEBREWS 12:3

Consider Him, the Lord of all!
    Consider Him, who gave the call
That sent you to that distant shore
    To do His work in Ecuador.

Consider Him, what He endured!
    Consider Him, and rest assured
That all He did and all He gave
    Would many, many sinners save.

Consider Him, who bids you go
    To tell to those who do not know
About the Savior's great concern
    For those who wait for your return.

Consider Him, whose loving heart
    Will comfort you when you depart,
And may our parting words conceal
    The loss and emptiness we feel.

Consider Him, who spoke and said,
  "Go tell, and let my sheep be fed."
Consider Him, who bids us pray
  For all your needs along the way.

Consider Him, as we unite
  To help you spread the Gospel light,
And as you go and we remain,
  May we together blessings gain.

Consider Him, the price He paid,
  The promise and the pledge He made:
That He will not forsake His own
  Who go to make His message known.

Bert Sundberg (Written, September 23, 1962;
sent to Evelyn, December 11, 1964.)

17

Patients and Patience

Evelyn's weeks took on a rhythm all their own. Tuesdays and Thursdays she visited house to house around Agato or trekked to outlying areas. Mondays, Wednesdays and Fridays were clinic days. On Wednesday, the big clinic day, Dr. Marcelo Endara came up from Otavalo. Indians came from all over the slopes of Taita Imbabura to seek help for themselves or sometimes even for their pig, or dog, or chicken or burro.

Most Spanish doctors would have had no time to give to such a clientele as this. After all, everyone knew that Indians were worthless! But since Marcelo had committed his life to Christ, a love for all persons had been infused into his nature. It was the love of the Lord Jesus Christ that was being demonstrated through him.

One day Dolores, who usually tended the clinic, was not feeling well, so Evelyn took her place. One of the most difficult tasks was to screen the patients during the morning hours, deciding which ones could be treated immediately and which ones would see Dr. Endara later. It was a great challenge to interpret symptoms properly: "My liver has been shivering a lot lately." (What on earth does that mean? Was it really their liver or . . . ?) "The last few days some little demons have been running around in my head." (A headache? Perhaps hallucinations?)

Roberto's deep gash was not healing well. It had been inflicted during a drunken brawl. Perhaps there should be stitches, not just bandages. Marcelo had better decide that.

Rafael complained of not being able to hear well. There was no equipment to test hearing, but the standard approach was to wash out the patient's ears. As usual, the amount of debris was phenomenal—a dirty, black substance—probably a combination of wax, soot and dirt. Fires burn in the Indians' mud-walled, windowless homes without any chimney. The smoke eventually seeps out through the thatched roof, but much of it lingers, meandering around the room, searching for an escape route. Such pollution did not afford the healthiest environment.

While Evelyn was diagnosing the patients' ills, the people congregated in the open-air "waiting room." The long wooden bench ran along the side of the house just outside the kitchen door. On Wednesdays, the day Dr. Endara visited the clinic, it was not long enough. Some patients stood, leaning against the chain-link fence. Others squatted in the shade of the house or a nearby eucalyptus tree. All of them were within earshot of the lean-to clinic. Evelyn could easily summon the next patient.

"Mama Michi," Evelyn called. An Indian woman approached with a small pig cradled in the loosely slung fachalina which hung from her neck and one shoulder. She was suckling the piglet at her own breast.

"The pig has been very sickly," she explained. "Please give it a needle! I was helped so much by the needle you gave me last week. I am sure it would help my pig, too."

Evelyn tried to explain that she didn't know anything about treating animals, but the woman was insistent.

Evelyn remembered how Carol Conn had once treated a sick chicken. She had crushed a sulfa pill and mixed the powder with some water. Somehow she got it down the throat of the chicken. The fowl recovered and Carol had gained a satisfied customer.

As Evelyn prepared a concoction for the piglet, her ear caught the words of Mama Manuela as she gave the Bible lesson to the waiting room crowd. Mama was getting very old and wrinkled now and a little bit confused at times as well. Evelyn overheard her as she came to a crucial point in the story of Jonah. "The passengers in 'the car'," she said, "wanted to throw Jonah into the lake, but the 'taxi driver' objected to such inhumane treatment."

It was too much for Evelyn. Here she was, an intelligent white woman mixing sulfa for a sick pig being suckled at a woman's breast, and listening to a spurious account of a taxi cab driver's defense of Jonah! Yes, Irene Downing was right. A good sense of humor was a basic requirement for missionary service.

Another facet of Evelyn's life that often tested her sense of humor was her car. The frustrations in that area were not always so laughable.

One day, at the end of her patience, Evelyn wrote the following letter to the field chairman, Bruce Jackson:

Dear Bruce,
Along with this quarterly report on the Toyota, I would like to make mention of a few things.

The mileage gauge is stuck at 126,999.

The gas gauge has never worked and sits on "E" all the time. So right now I don't know how many miles I have driven nor how much gas is in the tank.

The windshield wipers have always been temperamental and always give trouble in a rain storm. You may see me with a window open trying to get the wipers moving with a stick. Or you might see me pulled off the road to try to get them started from the side where they've stopped.

I have always had trouble getting the Toyota into reverse, but since Dick Fregeau worked on it some time ago, I'm having less trouble. Trouble, yes, but more often than not I can get it into reverse.

The brakes. On my way to Salasaca . . .

But let me describe the load Evelyn was carrying to Salasaca before the letter continues. The non-human load included a projector, several musical instruments and bedding and clothing for 13 people. Then there were the 13 people. In the cab (designed to seat four), there were five in the front seat and four, plus luggage, in the back. Another four rode behind the cab.

. . . nothing happened the first time. That was scary. However, I found out that by hitting them twice they would catch. I stopped at Dick Fregeau's and he tightened them up.

The carburetor is going bad and three times I got stalled. Once it was on a back road in Indian territory. Another time it was around Lake San Pablo in Imbabura. Again it was on my way to Ambato.

The oil gauge flickers almost constantly. It gave me quite a scare. However, that was faulty wiring and it has been taken care of for the moment.

> *The wiring to the starter gives trouble*
> *now and then. It is hard to get at it. I*
> *almost need to be in work clothes to fix*
> *it. I know the place to reconnect it on the*
> *lower part of the engine.*
>
> *The motor runs well, but it does not*
> *have much pickup and I have to take*
> *many of the hills in low gear.*
>
> *The Toyota is very hard riding. It*
> *shakes you like a bowl full of jelly.*
> *Because of the open back, when it rains I*
> *have to cover things and people with a*
> *large plastic sheet.*
>
> *I don't want to complain, but it would*
> *surely be a treat to have a suburban or a*
> *van. It would make it a lot easier to*
> *itinerate to such places as Cachijolla,*
> *Peguche, Quichinchi, Morochos and many*
> *other places in the province.*
>
> *Enough of that! Perhaps the Lord has*
> *something else in store for me.*

One of Evelyn's colleagues, reflecting upon
the vehicles she drove over the years, said,
"Perhaps the reason she was not given better
vehicles was that on those river beds, railroad
tracks and trail/roads, even a good vehicle
would have been turned into another rattle-
trap within three months."

"An overworked guardian angel!" That was
chairman Bruce Jackson's term for the unseen
being who traveled with Evelyn. To put it mildly, Evelyn was quite fearless in her approach to

the road! A number of incidents in Evelyn's life prompted Bruce's observation.

One day, she was enroute to Quito alone in the heat of the day. By bus, the trip could take about five hours. With Evelyn at the wheel, it could be done in three and a half hours.

The trip to Quito was a recurring necessity for various reasons—dental work at Salomon Cabeza's office, medical appointments, embassy business or vehicle repairs at Dick Fregeau's especially-for-missionaries garage. Evelyn often included a stop at the Christian bookstore and at the Bible Society where she would replenish her supplies.

There were always enjoyable occasions like eating at nice restaurants. La Fuente was a favorite with the missionaries. It had real class, at least by Ecuadorian standards. Then, there was always Kentucky Fried Chicken and a donut shop that rivaled Mister Donut.

Evelyn was rarely in Quito for a weekend, but when she was, she enjoyed attending the English Fellowship Church. It was attended by hundreds of North Americans who served with Radio Station HCJB, the Gospel Missionary Union, the Covenant Mission, her own Mission (The Christian and Missionary Alliance) and others. Only those who have been deprived of the joy of fellowship in their own language can imagine the emotions such an experience elicits.

Evelyn always stopped at the supermercado which bore considerable resemblance to the supermarkets back home. At the price of most things, however, Evelyn could wait till furlough time to enjoy such luxuries.

Then there was her friend Lois Hultberg, a sixth-grade teacher at the Alliance Academy. Lois was a fellow Minnesotan with Swedish roots. She regularly invited Evelyn to her apartment for a meal. It was a time Evelyn always looked forward to.

Carlos Remache, an Indian convert from Agato, often accompanied Evelyn on the return trip to Imbabura. He had sold all his ponchos and mantas at his little street stall. Evelyn was always glad to have him along. It was an additional opportunity to disciple Carlos. His help would be welcome, too, should the Land Rover give trouble along the road.

This time, however, Evelyn was alone as she headed to Quito. The miles of hairpin turns had kept her awake during the first part of the journey, but now, the wider, beautifully-paved Pan American highway posed a hazard. It seemed almost (yawn) boring!

Evelyn battled the tendency to let her eyelids drop, but it was getting more and more difficult to stay awake. After a couple of head jerks, she decided that it was time to get out and take a walk.

Unfortunately, her decision came too late. The vehicle slammed into the side of the stone face of the mountain and turned upside down, wheels spinning in the air.

Evelyn found herself lying on the roof of the car. Afraid that the vehicle might catch fire, she frantically searched for the nearest way out. The windshield was shattered, but it was too jagged to crawl through. One side of the vehicle, she observed, was tight against the rock face of the mountain. No exit that way. She tried to get the back seat loose, but remembered that the back was locked anyway. Only one door remained. She managed to open it and crawled out.

It took a few moments to get her bearings. Her eyes glanced to the opposite side of the road. To her horror, she saw a dropoff so precipitous that it would surely have been the end of her if she had gone over that side.

"Thank you, Lord," she breathed.

Evelyn knew that if she left the vehicle, there would be nothing left worth returning to. She asked passing motorists to carry word of the accident to the Alliance office in Quito.

Another incident happened the following April, only two days before Evelyn was to leave Ecuador. It was the same road, but a different spot.

As Evelyn rounded a curve, suddenly a large truck loomed in front of her. She slammed on the brakes. There was no traction on the mist-covered pavement. Her vehicle skidded across the road and slammed into the side of the mountain with a resounding thud. Once again, on the opposite side of the road, a steep drop, with no guardrails for protection, would have meant certain death.

And then there was the trip to La Libertad with a busload of young people.

As the bus careened down the road, one of the young people, Galo Loza, offered to exchange seats with Señorita Evelina so that she would have a better view of the countryside. Evelyn thanked Galo for his thoughtfulness, but declined the offer.

Moments later, the bus left the road, cartwheeled down an embankment and rolled three times. When Evelyn finally regained consciousness, she noticed that her own face was skinned, her clothes torn and the blood of others was liberally splattered over her. She had landed between the steering wheel and the top of the bus which had been severed from the body. Near her lay Galo Loza. As one of the front seat passengers, he had not fared well. With every heartbeat, blood spurted out of his mouth and the back of his head. He died.

Despite the accident, the bruised and battered survivors conducted services at La Libertad. People came from far and near to hear them testify. Many came to Christ.

It did seem to be true, as Bruce Jackson said, that Evelyn indeed had a guardian angel, an overworked one at that.

18

Amen, Jerry! Amen!

The garishly-painted Ecuatoriana Airlines Boeing 707 raced down the long runway. It seemed like minutes passed before Evelyn felt the plane hesitantly lift into the air. She remembered that planes needed lots of runway because of the thin air at the nearly two-mile-high Quito airport.

It was furlough time again. Evelyn was looking forward to being back home, although it was debatable where home was. Wherever Evelyn's body might be, her heart would always be in Imbabura. The long flight from Quito to Miami would be a welcome respite from the hectic final days.

Evelyn stared out the window. The crystal clear air made it easy to identify the magnificent snow-capped peaks of Cotopaxi, Antisana and Cayambe.

But the mountain she really wanted to see was Imbabura. The big plane banked sharply to the right as if to avoid collision with a peak. Actually, that was precisely the reason the pilot veered, for Quito is surrounded by high mountains. The plane pulled back to the left.

Suddenly, Taita Imbabura appeared. The giant, blue, valentine-shaped heart etched on its side brought instant tears to Evelyn's eyes. That's where she was leaving her heart!

Oh, how she loved those dear Quichua people to whom the Lord had sent her. She had faithfully carried the gospel to them. She wanted to see them delivered decisively from the terrible bondage in which Satan had held them for too long. There were some small encouragements, but the breakthrough she longed for had not been forthcoming. A faint sadness clouded her usually sunny countenance.

Evelyn reached into her carry-on bag and pulled out Jerry Conn's recent annual report to the field conference.

"We are amazed at the unapproachability of the Otavalo Indian," he had written. "This cold aloofness stands in sharp contrast to the warm friendliness of the jungle Indian. It is the number one cause for the slowness in reaching these Indians. Our fondest desire would be to report that the Agato church has a need for expansion. We are sad to say that there is no such need as yet, for it continues to flounder in its half-hearted, self-contented ways. Church and Sunday school are at about the same level (25-40). At the end of September, we were privileged to have the Gospel Missionary Union Quichua worker from Colta for services. There were no decisions for Christ. We were disappointed at the lack of cooperation and the indifference toward these services on the part of the church members.

"July marked the end of the Agato school. The committee of the Mission ruled that in accordance with the Policy and Procedures Book which states that 'the Mission shall not maintain schools where government schools are in the area,' the Agato school should not reopen the ensuing school year."

Jerry had gone on to report that because the parents had no confidence in the government school, many of the students now did not even attend school. A few went to the Catholic school. "A very wonderful and direct means of contact with these children and young people has been lost," he pointed out.

"Regular church attendance has continued about the same with an occasional visitor coming in. Sunday evenings . . . when we show slides or moving pictures we may expect between 50 and 60. When we have a Bible lesson, as few as three or four. There are frequently more outside than inside. They stand ready to push away those who attempt to enter the door or fight with the girls. Sometimes they play a serenade on their flutes or throw stones as we are trying to give the lesson. (Those stones, landing on the corrugated metal roof made a horrible noise.)

"There are absolutely no young men with any interest in spiritual things. No young men attending services. No one to help in the work."

Evelyn lingered over one sentence particularly: "One of the greatest needs is a lively group of born-again young people to lead in aggressive activity to reach the lost."

"You're right, Jerry!" Evelyn almost said it out loud.

Although much of the report painted a rather dismal picture of the situation at Agato, it was certainly not all negative. No indeed! Jerry concluded by urging, "Let's not pull out and say [the situation] is impossible until we have invested more honest labor mingled with earnest faith. Let us heed the counsel of Caleb and Joshua who said, 'If the Lord delight in us, then He will bring us into this land, and give it to us!'"

In her heart Evelyn knew what God could do. She thought about what fellow-missionary Jake Klassen had noted in his report: "Even the leadership in the Agato church sometimes get drunk, and then repents and is restored for a while, then falls into drinking again."

Yes, she knew it was all true. What they needed were some thorough conversions that would be a living testimony to God's ability to deliver from bondage.

"Oh God," she prayed, "help me to challenge the people I will minister to while on furlough. Having a host of prayer partners could make a difference, couldn't it, Lord?"

Of course it could! She knew that.

And it would!

Good old Minnesota! There were warm greetings from the welcoming party and the adjustment of mental pictures of friends and relatives to the reality of four years of separation.

There were wonderful firsts—like daring to drink out of a water fountain again and picking up the phone and getting through immediately. Both were absolute luxuries.

There was the pleasure of buying an apple without feeling guilty about the exorbitant price and marveling at the choices in the supermarket. Evelyn had never seen such a vast array of food.

There was the recurring challenge of knowing what she wanted to say, but having to translate it in her own mind from Spanish into English— a most frustrating linguistic exercise.

And then there were the challenges of putting together her slide presentations (who but the experienced can appreciate the hours it takes to accomplish that feat?) and sometimes not being allowed to minister in certain ways because she was a woman.

Pleasures. Adjustments. Frustrations. Challenges. Those seem to be the things that furloughs are made of.

The highlight of Evelyn's furlough turned out to be a week at Big Sandy Camp in McGregor, Minnesota. The speaker was Rev. James McFadden. His messages were direct and powerful, with a strong emphasis on the work of the Holy Spirit in the life of the believer.

Evelyn had been filled with the Spirit much earlier in her Christian experience, but now she felt a deep need for a new infilling that would bring wonderful results both inwardly and outwardly. New empowerment for unprecedented results. That's what she needed.

Evelyn asked Pastor McFadden to pray for her. Quietly, sincerely, he prayed that God would do a new and powerful thing in her life, for His own sake.

"Evelyn, things are going to be different for you back in Ecuador this next term," Pastor McFadden said as he finished his prayer. His words came as the voice of God to Evelyn's heart. A new spirit of expectation flooded over her and the rest of her busy days at home were lived in anticipation of what the Lord would do back in Agato.

"If the Lord delight in us, then He will bring us into this land, and give it to us."

Amen, Jerry! Amen!

19

Breakthrough

T*hese jets must be 25 years old,* Evelyn thought as she caught a glimpse of the waiting plane through the airport window. *I wonder if they ever replace them or do old planes never die—they just crash one by one?* She chuckled under her breath and walked briskly to her seat.

A gaudily dressed American woman occupied the seat next to hers. She gave no indication that she wanted to talk. While Evelyn was by and large uninhibited, she certainly was not forward. She settled back to relax and think. The last few weeks had allowed precious little time for either.

It was 1972. This was going to be a wonderful term. She could feel it. God had done something new for her in her spirit and surely this was to be passed along to others. The letters she had received from Imbabura while on furlough had given no hint of a much-prayed-for breakthrough, but she was certain that one was in the making. She looked forward to settling back into the heart of Imbabura Province as quickly as possible. By the time the plane

arrived in Quito, Evelyn had planned her re-
entry to the minutest detail.

"Evelyn," the field chairman announced
shortly after greeting her at the airport, "there
has been a change of plans. You will not be
going immediately to the Otavalo/Agato area.
We need you for a few months in the Mission
office. We will send you back to Imbabura
Province as soon as possible, but for now we
need some help right here."

A prayer-sigh escaped Evelyn's lips.

*Oh, Father? How does this fit into my spiritual
preparation for ministry? Is it necessary to be filled
anew with the Spirit to do bookkeeping?* A wave of
disappointment swept over her.

The few months in Quito were certainly not
Evelyn's first choice. In fact, her will had needed considerable realignment in order to accept
the position graciously. But they were a part of
the discipline of the Lord. And, yes, one does
need the fullness of the Spirit—even for office
work.

After three months, Evelyn was given the
green light to return to her beloved Imbabura.
Excerpts from her prayer letter reveal the mixed
feelings which accompanied the move:

> *I've enjoyed driving a little English
> Austin, but will soon be driving a Land
> Rover again.*
> *I've enjoyed all the luxuries of life in
> Quito with a lovely apartment, running*

*water, both hot and cold, and electricity
24 hours a day. Soon I will be in the
country where we have electricity from a
light plant only at night for a few hours,
outdoor bathroom facilities, etc.*

*I've enjoyed being in the office. Now, I
return to direct evangelism among Indians
where reception to the Gospel is very slow.
But I'm believing God for a break among
them.*

*Can I count on you to pray? Much
prayer is needed. Many are ready to
shake the dust from their feet and go
elsewhere. The jungle is much more attractive (God is greatly working there) yet I
see 100,000 Indians going to Christless
graves, steeped in darkness and sin and
in need of the light of the Gospel in the
province of Imbabura.*

*Am I to leave them for a more glam-
orous place? A place where things are
moving, where there is a much larger
staff for many less people?*

*An obscure Indian village may be a
great place—if it is the place of His will
and lit up with His presence.*

One day Evelyn struck upon an idea. What
about gospel recordings in the language of the
people? Could it be possible that music and
messages would touch the hearts of these seem-
ingly disinterested Indians?

Evelyn knew the power of music. It had been a part of her ministry ever since she had played and sung for street meetings in Little Falls as a teenager. What would happen, she wondered, if she would form a music ministry team with the Indians themselves? Would it have any effect? Would the crowds be better? Would music be the spark that could light a fire in Imbabura?

It wasn't long until a group was formed, for Evelyn was not one to dawdle. The group called themselves The INCAS.

Within a year, The INCAS had become the most famous Christian singing/playing group in all of Ecuador. Others caught on to the idea and formed their own teams. A new wave of Christian music ministry spread throughout all of Ecuador.

Evelyn and Mama Manuela became a team too, crisscrossing Imbabura together—Mama Manuela carrying the "box" (record player) on her back, and Evelyn walking behind her with the supply of gospel literature, used Christmas cards and her Bible.

"Lend me your path!" Evelyn would call out as they approached a mud-walled, thatch-roofed home.

"I lend you my path," would come the soft answer.

Evelyn often found the Indian women squatting in their bare yard, shelling corn. She and Mama Manuela would squat beside them and shell corn too.

"Would you like to see what this box can do?" they would ask. "Would you like to hear some music?"

"Oh yes!" came the reply. It was always the same positive answer. Evelyn placed a record on the player, wound it up and released the turntable. The women's dark eyes opened wider and wider as they heard first music and then a message in their own language.

God had shown Evelyn one way to break through to the Indian heart. Perhaps He had a plan for Imbabura after all.

Another factor in the breakthrough in Imbabura was the conversion of Dolores and Carmen Morales, sisters who had attended the Mission's grade school before it was closed by committee action. In fact, Dolores had been the first girl to graduate from the school. In the Indian mind, a girl did not need to be educated. Neither bearing children nor bearing burdens required a formal education, so why bother?

Dolores had continued her education and was now a practical nurse employed by the government to work among her own people. The first Indian nurse in Imbabura, she was highly respected and became known throughout the province for her good works.

There had never been, however, a clear-cut conversion on the part of either Dolores or her sister. Even with persistent witness and visitation by various missionaries, the girls had not responded to the gospel. They were good living people, better than most Indians by far. They would tell you that. They did not sense a need.

At about the same time that Dolores began to work in Imbabura, Antonio Velasquez came to minister with Evelyn as a lay pastor. Antonio had become a Christian while working at a factory in Quito. Not long after his conversion, Antonio's little boy died. Antonio decided that, rather than expending his energies on his own grief, he would dedicate his life to Christian service. So he offered his services as a minister of the gospel among his own people.

So serious was Antonio about this commitment that all on his own he completed 13 courses (88 lessons) of Bible study. He then went on to take other correspondence courses and even attended the Jungle Bible Institute for Indians in the Oriente (the Amazon basin jungle area of Ecuador), far from his mountain home.

Antonio was a diligent witness. What he may have lacked in training he made up for in holy boldness. One day, Antonio visited Dolores and Carmen Morales and received the same rationalizations that Carol and Evelyn had heard so often. Antonio had a ready reply.

"You are playing right into the hands of the devil," he told them. "It is true that you are not bad, but you are definitely lost."

The following Sunday both young women

were in the little church. Antonio's direct
approach must have had an impact, for both
Dolores and Carmen responded to his message and were saved.

"My sister and I went to church the Sunday
following a visit from Antonio Velasquez,"
Dolores testifies. "Something in that message,
and the words left in our home during that
week, made us tremble. I realized that all my
goodness in the home—obedience to my parents, helping people in the vicinity and now
even being prominent as a practical nurse—
none of those things brought me the satisfaction
I was looking for. For the first time in my life I
realized that I was a sinner, and that Jesus was
the only way. As I accepted Him, peace came to
my heart, joy filled my soul and everything
was changed. The heaviness was gone. The
trees seemed greener. The day was brighter."

Three people followed the Lord in the first
baptismal service ever held in Agato: Dolores,
Carmen and Antonio's own mother. What a
joyous occasion it was!

From the beginning of her conversion it was
evident that Dolores was a different kind of
believer from the ones that had made up the
church body in earlier years. She was thoroughly converted and exhibited a great hunger
for truth. As soon as Evelyn would teach her
something from the Bible, she would tell it to
others. Her sincerity and commitment were
very evident and very deep.

The government wanted to transfer Dolores to another area where she would work with the nuns. Not wanting to go, Dolores approached Evelyn about coming to work at the Agato clinic.

"I would love to have you, Dolores," Evelyn said, "but you are earning 600 sucres a month and we cannot afford to pay you that."

"How much could you pay me?" Dolores asked.

Evelyn thought for a moment and then replied, "Perhaps 400 sucres." Dolores did not flinch. "I will plan, then, to work here with you."

What a team! Antonio Velasquez (obviously gifted), Dolores Morales (intelligent, sincere, respected) and Conchita Lanchimba, an unpolished jewel from Morochos who had come to work for Evelyn as a maid. Conchita had only a third grade education, but she was exceptionally intelligent and she loved the Lord. She learned quickly and soon became a partner with Dolores in her evangelism efforts.

After more than 50 years of seed-sowing, the light was beginning to shine in Imbabura. Harvest time was coming to Agato.

Evelyn and her team of three Indians put concerted effort into the Evangelismo a Fondo (Evangelism in Depth) program. They taught the believers how to reach out to their own communities. The first time they announced hut-to-hut visitation, 22 people showed up.

More than 200 Indian homes were visited that first Sunday.

Follow-up was done faithfully. Wind-swept villages high on the spine of the Andes welcomed the teams as they came with medicine and with the gospel. Prayer cells quickly turned into house churches.

In one year, the team visited 1,020 homes. More than 12,000 tracts and booklets were distributed. Seventy-five Bibles and 300 New Testaments were sold. One hundred and two people made decisions for Christ. There were numerous baptisms—15, then another 31, then 51 more, then 90, then over 100 in that fifth baptism. It was evident that the lives of these new believers were being powerfully changed. The bondage of liquor was broken. There was a deep desire to share the good news with others. God was finally breaking through in response to earnest prayer and years of faithful planting and watering.

Campaigns were scheduled in the larger centers of Imbabura Province. Before the services, Indian believers marched through the streets, parade-like, toward the place where the meeting was to be held. Evelyn played her guitar or accordion. Someone else wielded an electrified bull horn announcing what the parade was all about. The pastor played his mandolin. Others followed playing a variety of instruments.

Then a crowd would gather behind them, and like the pied piper, Evelyn and her team would lead the procession into the tent or stadium for the service. A people's movement was gaining momentum. Or would it be better to call it a Holy Spirit movement?

Mike and Carol Welty came to join Evelyn in the work. They were both well suited for the task in the Otavalo/Agato area. Their training and experience rounded out the team effort.

The Weltys' outfit had mysteriously disappeared en route to Ecuador, so, for the first six months, they lived with Evelyn in the big Mission house. When they finally discovered where their belongings were, they found out that the bill of lading had somehow become separated from the shipment. The customs official, thinking their goods were contraband, had placed them under lock and key.

During those days together, Evelyn and the Weltys discussed the new beginnings of the church in Imbabura Province. It was decided that radio broadcasts would be a good way to reach the Indians. The programs should be all-Indian. That decision proved to be most significant, for the "new religion," as some were calling it, became known as a religion of the Indians, not one associated with foreigners.

Dolores and Antonio did most of the speaking on the radio programs. Other believers provided music. Radio Station HCJB in Quito heard about the broadcasts. With their assistance, the one-hour a week program in Imbabura turned into eight hours aired throughout all of Ecuador, Peru and Bolivia.

Evelyn and her co-workers were overjoyed as they watched what God was doing. An ever-increasing number of Indians were seeing the rainbow for what it really was: God's wondrous promise of blessing and reassurance that He would never again allow what He had previously permitted.

Satan would never again control uncontested the slopes of Taita Imbabura. His reign of terror was over! The breakthrough had come!

20

If a Grain of Wheat...

In the providence of God, two elderly Indian women also became key factors in the breakthrough in Imbabura. The significance of their contribution could not have been predicted.

In spite of her declining mental capacity, Mama Manuela had consistently been the one truly bright spot in the darkness which surrounded Imbabura.

The Conns had given her a bedroom in the Mission house to which she could come whenever she wished to pray. There, behind closed doors, they could often hear Mama weeping and crying out to God for her beloved Indian people.

She had, through the years, guided Evelyn and others along familiar trails to homes where there was need for medicines and, of course, the gospel. Always the gospel. Along the trails, before passing a house, Mama Manuela would stop abruptly and pause to pray for its inhabitants. As they walked, Mama Manuela would stoop to pick up twigs, dried leaves and slivers of wood for her little fire that evening. With

both limited wood and limited lighting fuel,
she would squat by the fire and pray out loud:
"Oh, my Father, let my pot boil quickly before
my fire goes out!"

Over many years Mama Manuela came daily
to the Mission house to help in any way she
could. She ground coffee, husked corn, swept
the kitchen floor or weeded the garden. Always
it had been done for the Lord.

On clinic days Mama Manuela was always
there with her chart depicting the two ways, the
one leading to heaven, the other to hell. Every
person who came for "curations" (Howard
Cragin's term) had received spiritual medicine
first from the lips of Mama Manuela. The dis-
tortions of details in those last years did not
seem to obscure the message of the gospel that
flowed from her loving heart.

Mama Manuela did not live long enough to
fully understand that her prayers for Imbabura
were beginning to be answered. In her heart she
knew that God had heard her, but her physical
eyes never saw the great harvest that eventually came. That joy became hers on October 2,
1972, when Mama Manuela was promoted to
heaven. The spiritual breakthrough began that
very year!

Mama Juana Espinoza started attending the
church in Agato. A widow with three grown
daughters, Juana responded to the gospel message and was thoroughly converted. Evelyn
was greatly encouraged by the faithfulness of

this new convert.

At Pucará, where she lived, Mama Juana talked about the Lord to anyone who would listen. Some of her neighbors were greatly opposed to evangelical truth and threatened her with violence if she continued to share her faith. Juana told Evelyn and Antonio that if she were ever missing from church, they should suspect foul play and come looking for her.

A few weeks later, Mama Juana missed prayer meeting. She also missed the following Sunday's meetings. Remembering what Mama Juana had told him, Antonio went to her house. He found it ransacked and stripped of everything. Mama Juana was nowhere to be found. No one, apparently, had heard anything. No one had seen anything. Mama Juana had simply disappeared.

Antonio organized a search party. Believers from Otavalo came to help with the search. Evelyn and the police also came. They finally found her body in a ravine, partially covered with dirt and badly decomposed. Dogs had been eating the exposed flesh.

Some of the believers pooled their resources and bought a casket. They put it in a pickup and went to the ravine. No one wanted to touch the body, but the loving hands of Juana's fellow believers eventually did what no one else would do. They lifted her decaying body into the casket and then up on top of Mike Welty's suburban. The stench was too bad to put it inside. The body was taken to the morgue

in Otavalo for an autopsy, but the health officer
ruled that it was too decomposed for an autopsy. He gave the believers the papers for burial.
Disinfectant was poured over the body and
masked believers brought it to Agato. There,
Mama Juana's body was buried in the evangelical cemetery.

About a week later, an Indian, bellowing
brazenly in his drunken state, threatened all
evangelicals with the same thing he had done to
Mama Juana. The evangelicals in Pucará,
though deeply troubled, remained faithful in
their witness. Other villagers came to Christ.
The little house church soon became too small
to hold the crowds.

The fledgling church dreamed of having their
own building. It was a dream that would come
true. A piece of land was donated. Plans were
formulated for a building that would seat 400-
500. Sucres were carefully accumulated until
the believers felt they could start to build. A
contractor was engaged for only $15,000 for
the entire job. Laborers volunteered to help
without cost. Women cooked for the workers.

Within weeks, the walls were ready for the
roof, but there were no funds for the roof.
About that time, a tour group came through the
area. One man wanted to give $1,000 to some
project among the Indians. Evelyn decided it
should go for the roof at Pucará. The donation
not only paid for the roof, but it was also
enough to paint the sanctuary and buy benches.

What a joyful dedication service was held at Pucará when the building was finally completed! The beautiful sanctuary was filled with believers from all of the surrounding communities. The congregation sang "There is no God as great as my God," and "We praise Thee, O God" and "How Great Thou Art." Thirteen churches sent musical groups for special numbers. Officials of The Christian and Missionary Alliance were there to bring greetings. It was a marvelous day.

The building had cost 484,850 sucres (about $12,000). God had provided it all. In one baptismal service after another more were added to the church. The Pucará church continued to grow rapidly, 100, 120, 140, 150. In 1991, there were 250 persons attending the church at Pucará.

. . . unless a kernel of wheat falls to the ground and dies, it remains only a single seed. But if it dies, it produces many seeds. (John 12:24)

21

Their Own Mushuj Testamento

With such an influx of new converts in Imbabura, the matter of discipleship became a priority. Evelyn was well aware that proper foundations for spiritual growth include a Bible and a hymnbook. She was deeply committed to the production of both.

The little mimeographed hymnal they were presently using was far from adequate. Evelyn and Carol Conn took it upon themselves to revise and augment it. It was an enormous job. The language structure made it extremely difficult. Long words had to be fitted to music as smoothly as possible. The following lyrics indicate something of the challenge that Carol and Evelyn faced:

Pai nanaihuan cashpa, yacunaiyan, nirca.
Chai gentecunaca vinagreta curca.
Shuj shuhua runaca Jesusta manarca
Arrepentirishpa; perdonahuai, nirca.
Chai shuhua runaman tigrachishpa nirca;
'Cunan punllallata cieloman rishunmi.'

Two hundred and fifty-one hymns and choruses were eventually collected into a bound hymnal. A later revision, made by Evelyn and Dolores Morales, incorporated new, indigenous hymns written by Indians for Indians.

The New Testament was another matter. It had taken months of laborious work to produce a hymnal. It would take years to finish the New Testament. Gunther Schulze, an independent translator, headed up the project. In order to make the Scriptures applicable to all, Indians from each region of Imbabura were hired as informants.

This practice sometimes made it difficult to find a word acceptable to all. For example, how do you translate "Holy Spirit" into a language where the word for spirit is always used for bad spirits? Shall it become the Holy Bad Spirit? Such linguistic idiosyncracies demanded hours and hours of collaboration and study.

Other Mission groups and denominations, including the Catholics, were invited in for the final revision. It was important that this New Testament be bought and used by all the Indians of the area. Broad acceptance, without compromise of the finished product, was the goal.

Paul Young represented the United Bible Societies in Ecuador. In fact, it could be said quite accurately that Paul Young *was* the Bible Society in Ecuador. He took a deep interest in the Quichua Bible and made numerous trips to

Agato during the translation process. The fact that he had long since retired and was now nearly 80 years of age made people admire him all the more. Evelyn hoped that she would have as much energy 25 years later when she was his age.

Seeing Paul Young again reminded Evelyn of the time that he had rescued her from Pascual Molino, the persistent suitor in Guayaquil, during her first term. Just think—she could have long since been Mrs. Molino. A slight smile wrinkled her eyes as she reviewed that scenario. She wondered whatever had happened to Pascual. He had not married a missionary, at least not a Christian and Missionary Alliance missionary. Of that she was certain.

Seeing Paul also reminded Evelyn of a most enjoyable tea that she and others had enjoyed in the Youngs' home in Quito when Bernice had been alive. Bernice was such a gracious hostess, their beautiful home an impressive setting for a formal tea.

It was fun to dress up once in a while. Everyone was dressed up, including Paul. He always had about him a statesman-like bearing— an almost British refinement such as accompanies a true gentleman. The enjoyment of the afternoon would never be forgotten. Fawcett was profoundly perceptive when he penned the words, "the fellowship of kindred minds is like to that above."

And now, to have Paul Young here in her

beloved Imbabura. It was an honor. He, along with the dedicated, faithful, persistent Gunther Schulze, became the hero of the team working on the New Testament. Paul raised the money for the Testament's publication and eventually hand-carried the completed manuscript to the New York Bible Society where he managed to have it included in the printing schedule for that very year.

The ever-increasing number of converts in Imbabura would soon have God's Word to read in their own language.

22

The Ultimate Serendipity

Evelyn would never forget the shock of it! Paul Young's visit itself was not so unusual. All the missionaries stopped by for a piece of rhubarb pie or some other freshly-made delicacy when they were in the area. They knew that the welcome mat was always out at Evelyn's place. No, what really shocked her about Paul's visit was the topic of conversation.

Paul handed Evelyn a box of candy. He was always doing thoughtful things for others. *That's nice of him*, Evelyn thought to herself. She not only loved candy—she also greatly respected this man of God.

Evelyn invited Paul into her little kitchen and pulled out a chair in the breakfast nook. Soon there were some freshly-baked cinnamon rolls on the table and Evelyn poured some hot tea.

"Evelyn," Paul began, "it has been six years since Bernice died. I have not wanted to approach anyone before, but . . . what would you think about getting married sometime?"

Evelyn was flabbergasted. Responses swirled through her mind. None of them seemed appropriate. Marriage? To Paul? The possibility had never even crossed her mind. After all, though he didn't seem to be, Paul was 25 years her senior.

Apparently anticipating that thought, Paul asked, "Evelyn, how old are you?"

She told him.

"I know there is a considerable age difference," he replied, "but I have just had a physical and my doctor tells me I have the body of a man 25 years younger. I think my lifestyle backs that up, too."

Paul's assertion was certainly undeniable. But there was another important factor to consider. What of her beloved Imbabura? What Paul did not seem to understand was that Evelyn was already married. Her heart belonged to Imbabura.

Finally regaining her composure, Evelyn began: "Why, Paul, that is very nice of you, but I have work to do here in Imbabura. My ministry among the Indians is too important for me to even think of getting married."

"Our marriage would not preclude that, Evelyn," Paul insisted. "You could continue doing exactly what you are doing and I could continue my work in connection with the Bible Society. I could work right along with you among your beloved Indians."

It was true what Paul said. They did have a lot in common. But marriage?

Evelyn needed time to think.

23

For Better or for Worse

It was an excited group of missionaries who saw Paul and Evelyn off at the Quito airport. Evelyn was deeply loved and respected by her colleagues. So was Paul. The single missionary ladies especially reveled in the sparkle that surrounded the new couple. They had followed each romantic detail with particular interest since the arrival of that first box of candy.

Neither Paul nor Evelyn seemed concerned about the age difference. They had long since settled that issue. Paul had certainly not aged through the years the way most men do. And, after all, "it is just history repeating itself," the older missionaries mused. They remembered how Homer Crisman had married Irene Downing who was more than 20 years younger than he. They lived many happy years together and he was well into his 90s before the Lord took him home.

One thing Paul and Evelyn both knew—they loved each other. Their union, they believed, would not hinder but rather enhance their work for the Lord. They felt in their hearts that God had brought them together. After all these years of knowing and respecting one another, their mutual admiration had blossomed into deep and genuine love.

The hours on the plane flew by as they talked of wedding plans, of their love for each other and of their love for Imbabura. In Miami Paul and Evelyn parted for separate destinations. In just a few weeks they would meet once again. That time, it would be at the Minneapolis/St. Paul airport when Paul arrived for the wedding. The anticipation of that occasion would enhance the days in between.

Evelyn busied herself with the wedding details and a whirlwind of activities. A special family dinner was planned to allow the relatives to get acquainted with Paul. Evelyn was sure that they would love him as she did, but she did have to admit that it was a little nerve-wracking. *It isn't all that different from a teenager bringing her new boyfriend home,* Evelyn thought to herself, and chuckled. Everyone who knew Paul loved and respected him. Why shouldn't her family?

The next big event was the groom's dinner. What a joy-filled occasion that was! The wedding party and selected guests gathered at The House of Wong. All the happy traditions were observed. Paul and Evelyn gave gifts to their attendants. Serious and not so serious speeches were made. Then everyone piled into cars and headed for Simpson Memorial Church.

The Rev. Carl Volstad, who had himself

served many years in South America, officiated at the rehearsal. There was the usual mixture of fun and confusion. The vows were repeated and repeated—"for better or for worse, for richer or for poorer, in sickness and in health." How many times had Evelyn heard them before? Tomorrow it would be a binding, heartfelt commitment of two people—herself and Paul—to each other. Nothing except death itself would nullify that commitment. Tomorrow held the promise of a beautiful, Christ-honoring wedding and the beginning of a partnership in life and ministry.

Evelyn looked at Paul. He seemed tired, but then, why shouldn't he be tired? She was tired too, come to think of it. These had been a hectic few weeks.

Evelyn checked the food preparations in the lower auditorium. Everything was in good hands, so Paul and Evelyn excused themselves and headed to her brother's car. Evelyn slid behind the wheel.

"I should be the one driving you," Paul mused. They laughed together at the role reversal. Evelyn would drop Paul off at her brother Phil's place and she would then drive on to Merle's for her last night as a single woman.

Our last night apart. Just think. By this time tomorrow I will be Mrs. Paul Young! Evelyn had waited a long time for this day.

The couple sat for a while in front of Phil's house. Though reluctant to part, Paul reached over and kissed Evelyn. They lingered in the embrace. Then Paul turned to get out.

Instead of reaching for the door handle, however, he just sat there, motionless. He didn't say anything. He just sat there.

What is he thinking? Is everything all right? Evelyn wondered to herself. *Why doesn't he open the door?* The questions tumbled through her mind.

"Paul! Are you all right?" Evelyn asked.

No response.

She raised her voice. "Paul!"

Again, no response.

"Paul," she repeated, "is something wrong?"

Still no answer.

Not wanting to leave him to run for help, Evelyn gave one long piercing blast on the horn. Her niece came dashing out of the house.

"Aunt Evelyn, is something wrong?"

"Yes, Becky, it's Uncle Paul. Quickly! Call for help!"

The next few hours were a nightmare blur of unexpected, frantic activity. The police arrived. They did not wait for the paramedics or an ambulance. Instead, they put Paul in their police car and rushed off to Ramsey Hospital.

Police. Emergency room. Doctors. Nurses. Relatives. Phone calls (outgoing). Someone to explain to guests at the door of the church. Cancel flowers. Friends. Initial diagnosis. Probing questions. Uncertain prognosis. Phone calls (incoming).

An assortment of unplanned activities replaced the carefully laid and nearly consummated plans of two people in love. Evelyn was in a state of shock. She stayed by Paul's side. She held his hand. She gave him what reassurances she could. She relayed messages from the many who called and wrote. Days passed, but Paul gave no verbal response.

While Paul battled the effects of the stroke, Evelyn was facing her own struggle. *Why?* The question muscled its way unbidden into her mind. But then, God doesn't prohibit that question, does He? Even the Lord Jesus asked it on the cross: "My God, my God, why hast thou forsaken me?" *Why, Lord? Why?*

As days became weeks, it became increasingly evident that the stroke had been a massive one. Even therapy, to which Paul gave his full cooperation, was accomplishing precious little. Evelyn stayed by Paul's side for two months— two long and difficult months for both of them. The sudden, dramatic change of plans was painful to accept, but these were two very dedicated servants of the Lord. A committed heart does not easily swerve from that position.

One day, Paul and Evelyn were sitting alone— Paul in his wheelchair, Evelyn on a chair beside him. It was time, she decided, to discuss their future. Carefully Evelyn went over all they had planned to do together. She reminded Paul that God had altered those plans by permitting the stroke. Then, speaking gently, she said, "Paul, I have two more years to go to complete this term of service. Do you think I should go back to Ecuador now?"

Evelyn knew how Paul's children felt about that issue. They had been most gracious.

"Evelyn," they had told her, "we do not expect you to take care of our father. We will see to that. He will have the best of care. We want you to feel perfectly free to make plans to return to Ecuador. We think Dad would want you to do that. We do not feel that you are abandoning him or going back on any promises by returning. Your engagement was a promise to marry Dad. It now appears that will never be possible. We want you to know how we feel and how we think Dad feels, too."

Paul answered Evelyn's question with a feeble "yes." He could say nothing more. Evelyn kissed him goodnight and left. Over and over her mind replayed the one-sided conversation. If only she could be certain that Paul had really understood what she was saying.

One day, when Paul seemed especially alert, Evelyn once more carefully reviewed the conversation of a few weeks earlier. This time, to her surprise, Paul asked, "What . . . do . . . you . . . want . . . to . . . do?"

"What do I want to do?" Evelyn asked, pointing to herself.

"Yes" he replied.

"I want to do the will of the Lord," she answered. Then she added, "What do you think

I should do? Should I return to Ecuador?"

"Yes," he said once more.

"There is a lot of work to do there yet, work we had hoped to do together," Evelyn continued.

"Yes," he repeated.

Yet a third time, some days later, Evelyn approached Paul with the same question. This time she specifically asked him, "Do you want me to stay at home here with you?" If Paul answered yes to that question as well, she would be back to square one.

"No," came the answer.

It was a confirmation to the continual tug of Evelyn's heart toward Imbabura. With it, Evelyn was convinced that she could with certainty say that both she and Paul wanted God and His work in Ecuador to have priority in their lives, even though it would not be easy for either of them.

In a lengthy letter to Paul's children, Evelyn closed the final paragraph by saying:

> *I've counted it all joy to be with Paul during these very difficult . . . months of illness and would love to continue. But time is running out and I'd better get back to my job. Farewells will not be easy, nor going back to Ecuador without Paul, but our God is sufficient and He will sustain, so do continue to pray.*

A heart for Imbabura and a heart for Paul Young too? Could that be possible?

Yes, it could be and it was. In fact, it could be said that Evelyn had a heart for God, a heart for Imbabura, and a heart for her beloved. A triune love.

God understands that. He is quite familiar with the triune concept.

24

No Time for Tears

Evelyn relaxed against the headrest as the big jet lifted off from Miami airport. It had been a trying few months for both Paul's family and her. Paul had settled in well to a beautiful nursing home in Florida. He would not lack for love and care.

For Evelyn, returning to Ecuador alone when dreams had planned it otherwise was a deep disappointment. How different the circumstances would have been if Paul's stroke had come 24 hours later. That thought had run through Evelyn's mind on more than one occasion.

But people do not control these things, Lord. You do. And I bow to Your sovereignty. The thought was a commitment both to herself and to God.

A pretty Ecuadorian stewardess leaned into the row ahead of her to ask what the passengers would like to drink. Before she could inquire at Evelyn's row, Evelyn said spontaneously, "Sprite, por favor. Gracias!"

Evelyn chuckled as she realized that just looking at the stewardess had prompted her to slip into Spanish. There was something about that that pleased her. She wasn't sure what it was. Maybe it was that she was heading home. Evelyn sipped her Sprite as her thoughts turned south. In many ways Quito was more familiar to her than Minneapolis.

Another mental leap landed her in Agato. Her mood lifted immediately as she thought of Dolores and Lucila and others who would be there to greet her.

Imbabura! Ah, yes. Now that was home! What all had happened throughout the province during the nearly three months she had been away? Had its heart softened even further? Had the light penetrated even more deeply?

The letters had been most encouraging. The movement of the Holy Spirit was continuing unabated, they said. Morochos was growing, too. Sixty-four in church and 11 candidates for baptism. Evelyn longed to see it all for herself. She wanted to be a part of it again.

One letter had said that there were 453 at an Indian service in Otavalo. Oh, how they needed the proposed new Center!

Very quickly Evelyn was back into the frenetic pace. The growing church needed much assistance to ensure that its foundations would be strong even if someday there were no resident missionary.

Before Paul and Evelyn had gone to the States for their wedding, the translation of the Quichua New Testament had been completed.

Now the galley proofs had arrived. For many weeks, at the folding table in Evelyn's kitchen, she and the local informants pored over the proofs. A pot of fresh coffee and some just-out-of-the-oven cinnamon rolls always helped. One read aloud while the others scrutinized the script to attempt to catch every spelling error. Gunther Schultze, the translator who had worked with Paul, was back in the States studying. Paul Young's part could be only intercessory prayer. The completion of the project was now in Evelyn's hands.

At last, with the galley proofs thoroughly checked and found to be in good order, the manuscript was returned to the printer. There was nothing to do but wait.

Finally, after what seemed like years (it was actually only a matter of months, thanks to Paul Young's earlier diligence), word came to Evelyn that the bound copies had arrived in Quito. June 5, 1977 was chosen as the dedication day. Preparations for the celebration took top priority for Evelyn and her colleagues. The Indians prepared invitations for town dignitaries, provincial officials, the governor and officials of The Christian and Missionary Alliance. Even the priests from Otavalo were invited.

The day dawned bright and clear. By 7:30 a.m., groups of Quichua Indians began arriving at the Mission house. From all over the province they came, singing and bearing banners embellished with both real and crepe paper flowers. A singing group from Quito arrived, wearing red, striped ponchos overslung with white shoulder shawls. The INCAS, the seven-member local group, were stunning in their aqua ponchos for the men and blue velvet skirts and shawls for the women. The Otavalo Municipal Band arrived in a special bus and marched onto the improvised platform. While the band played, all the other groups and delegations entered the compound behind their colorful banners. Agato was really on the map that day as 1,000 people squeezed into the Mission compound.

At 9:00 a.m. the band struck up the national anthem and a mass of Spanish voices joined in. Then, to most everyone's surprise, the choirs from the Otavalo and Agato Indian churches sang the anthem in their own language, Quichua. It was an emotion-laden beginning for the service.

Evelyn read greetings from Paul. One of the verses included in his letter was touchingly appropriate coming from a man who could not have spoken to them even if somehow he could have been wheeled onto the platform: "The grass withers, the flowers fade, but the Word of our God shall stand forever" (Isaiah 40:8 LB). Paul certainly had withered, but what he had helped to bring to fruition would never die—the Word of the Living God in Quichua.

Evelyn spoke briefly of the great contribution

Paul had made to the publication of the Quichua New Testament. The people responded with an enthusiastic ovation.

Washington Padilla, representing the United Bible Societies, presented the first copy of the New Testament to Antonio Otavalo, the president of the Regional Indian Committee. He in turn presented it symbolically to the Indian people.

The government official for the area made a very moving speech. He expressed deep appreciation for the impact of the gospel on the Indian people. Then he spoke like a true politician: "I am on the side of the Indian," he assured the assembled crowd. "There is no need to bring a lawyer when you come to me. I will see that you get justice. I treat the Indians like people when they come to me."

Even as the band was playing the opening anthem, Gunther Schultze's plane from California was passing over Imbabura en route to Quito. A car was waiting in Quito to spirit him off on the two-hour trip to Agato. His arrival near the end of the festivities provided a dramatic climax for the celebration. And what a blessed celebration it had been!

Within an hour after the close of the program, 400 copies of the New Testament were sold. Two hundred more were sold in the next two days. It was very moving to observe Indian believers excitedly sharing with one another the new discoveries they were making in their precious possession.

Eighty persons, including officials, Indian leaders, translators and informants, enjoyed a delicious banquet at the Mission house.

The celebration was complete. It had been a day of great rejoicing. The only tears were tears of joy that welled up in Evelyn's eyes when the crowd had so enthusiastically applauded Paul's greetings. With all her heart Evelyn wished he could be standing there beside her experiencing the exhilaration of this historic day. Now the Living Word could begin to have its profound effect on the Indian church in Imbabura. The thousands of hours of tedious and sometimes frustrating work would bear eternal fruit.

Epilogue

It's January 1991. Evelyn, at age 71, is back in Ecuador for the second time since her retirement. The indigenous Indian church of Imbabura has invited her for the dedication of their new church building in Agato on Good Friday, March 29th. They want Señorita Evelina to be there.

Let's take one last stroll around the Mission compound and consider what God has done here in Imbabura Province.

We're standing on the highest point on the property. It is probably the very spot where Homer Crisman stood and surveyed the surrounding countryside, his heart-burden for these Indians driving him into this hostile territory.

There was no resident Alliance missionary among the more than 100,000 spiritually destitute persons 80 years ago when Homer Crisman stood here. There is no resident Alliance missionary here now either.

But, oh the difference! They were lost and without hope in 1911. They are found and have been presented with a glorious hope in 1991. Today, there is a living, aggressive, indigenous church here, storming the strongholds of Satan and winning absolutely thrilling victories.

Here's the old mud-walled Mission house. Those walls are older than Evelyn by a few years. What stories they could tell! You and I have shared some of them.

Right there, that's the room in which Mama Manuela wept for her people. It is simple and unadorned, but I imagine it is precious to God, a sanctuary where He met with a plain, but believing Indian woman.

Evelyn shared that grand old house with at least six colleagues through the years. Hundreds of others spent a night or a few days with her. She should have kept a guest log, but in her mind, no doubt, there were more important things to do.

See that second-floor window? That's where the thieves threw clods of dirt when Evelyn shined the flashlight out the window. Now, she would chuckle at the memory, but it was no laughing matter back then.

We round the corner. There! That's the bell she rang with all her might in the middle of the night. Now that old bell regularly calls hundreds of worshipers to the new church. In the early days, as few as three people responded. On Good Friday, in just a few weeks, the bell may welcome as many as 1,000. Such a prospect was almost inconceivable back then.

See that building down the hill with lots of windows? That's the old school. The Mission closed it, but not before it had graduated a Dolores Morales who became a significant part of the team God used in Imbabura.

And over there, beyond the compound fence. Do you see that plain, mud structure with the clay tile roof? That's the cantina where the drunken Indians formed a human barricade in an effort to get Evelyn to stop and give them money. The enemy almost succeeded in getting rid of Evelyn that night.

The cantina is still in business, but it doesn't have nearly the clientele it used to. An ever-increasing number of Indians are being delivered from their drunkenness as they come to Christ. The cantina owners, though frustrated, don't even try to challenge the believers or attempt to pour liquor down their throats on their way to church anymore.

We nearly stumble over the stone that marks the grave of George LeFevre here on the front lawn. George invested his brief life in this place, you know. Come to think of it—so did Mama Juana. They gave their lives for Imbabura. God let them die for Imbabura. God let Evelyn live for Imbabura.

Just around the corner of the house we'll see the narrow passageway between the kitchen door and the chain link fence. This bench is where the Indians sit when they come to the clinic. This is where Mama Manuela had Jonah thrown into a lake over the protests of a taxi-driver!

If only Mama Manuela could be on the platform on Good Friday to see the 1,000 rejoicing converts! Perhaps she will view the proceedings from the grandstand of heaven and rejoice with them.

Rounding the back corner of the house, we

walk past the old light plant and through the
garden toward the new church building. It is
huge and imposing, capable of seating 700
comfortably, and 1,000 on special occasions.
Good Friday will be a special occasion!

The old church building squatted right where
this structure now sits. It didn't do much for
the image of the evangelicals. By contrast, this
new temple literally dominates the landscape. It
is unquestionably the most beautiful building
anywhere on the chest of Taita Imbabura, to the
glory of God.

Oh yes, Taita Imbabura. We turn our heads to
the right and look over the wall where the
thieves broke through. We want to see if Taita
Imbabura has removed the veil of clouds so
that we can view his beautiful head.

But instead, we see a rainbow—a brilliant
rainbow encircling the horizon! Oh, thank you,
Lord.

There is no sound of Indians beating on kettles. No one is pinching his dog's ears to make
him squeal in the hopes of driving the demons
away.

On the contrary. Most Indians now thrill to
see the rainbow. From being a symbol of the
diablo himself, God has caused the rainbow
once again to be a symbol of His faithfulness.
Things will never again be as they once were.
God has decreed it!

And under the rainbow? Why, there it is—the
deep-blue gigantic heart over which that multi-

colored arch presides. God cares about these people. Even before Homer Crisman made that difficult horseback ride, God cared about these people. His great heart of compassion vibrated with love for these oppressed, poverty-stricken, bereft, Satan-bound, high-mountain Quichua Indians. He was not and He is not willing that any one of them should perish.

Just last Sunday, 67 Indian converts were baptized down in Lake San Pablo. I ask you—where, in all of the United States or Canada, have that many people been baptized in one service lately?

"How great is our God!" Those are the sentiments Evelyn expressed in a letter that arrived from Ecuador just yesterday. It was God's own great compassionate heart of love that prompted Him to form an embryo in Freedhem, Minnesota, over 70 years ago.

That embryo developed into a very special woman—Evelyn Rychner—who truly had a heart for Imbabura!

Charles W. Shepson
January 1991

Afterword

The following is a letter, copied verbatim, from Azucena Ramirez Straughan, dated December 3, 1990:

"It is for me a privilege and honor to be able to write about her character and the work carried on for the Lord by a beloved friend and sister in Christ, Miss Evelyn Rychner.

"I knew Miss Rychner in the year 1950 in the city of Guayaquil, Ecuador when I was very young. I attended the Alliance Evangelical Temple. One day there appeared this young missionary, kind, friendly, full of energy, ready to cooperate in any activity of the church, especially with the young people.

"I was impressed with her great love for the Lord, her dedication to the work, and also her tenacity in the same. She demonstrated a great love for lost souls. She was full of enthusiasm and spiritual power. She went anywhere. It didn't matter the circumstances or conditions of the place or the persons. Her goal was to carry the gospel of salvation. In a way, Miss Rychner was my spiritual mother, my teacher. Accompanying her to all the different places and seeing her manner of life and work had a great influence on my life. I also decided to go prepare myself to work for our blessed Savior, Jesus Christ.

"I spent four years preparing myself, and when I graduated, she invited me to work with her in the city of Otavalo. Living in the same house with Evelyn confirmed that she was a real servant of God—a woman full of the Holy Spirit.

"The Lord took first place in her life. Evelyn is a well organized person. She does not waste time on things outside of the work the Lord has committed into her hands. She does more than her human strength allows. Many times I saw her tired, but not bored or lacking patience with anyone.

"Evelyn worked seven days a week, from the time she arose until the hour to retire. When she went to bed, she went with her books, to study. Mondays, which were supposed to be days of rest, she dedicated to visits and to the propagation of the gospel among the Indians who lived far off in the mountains. We would leave in the morning and return at nightfall, tired but full of happiness, knowing that we had carried the gospel to places where it had never entered before. If it had not been for her interest in the Indians, no one would have bothered.

"Evelyn was the director of construction of the chapel in those places, and she herself helped in the work. Her love for the people was sincere and not self-seeking. She was ready to help and to do well to anyone who needed it.

"Evelyn has a heart full of compassion. If someone came to the door at midnight for help or wishing that she take someone to the hospital because of illness, she would go out at that hour no matter what the distance, or how cold the night. The doors of her house were always open to people of any condition or social standing, or any race. She has a great love for the Indians.

"With her retirement Ecuador has lost a hero, a support! She was one of the best missionaries of the century.

"Thanks to God and to her for her life, her example, and her contribution to my country, Ecuador. We pray that God may raise up more missionaries with the same abnegation, zeal, and Holy Spirit's fullness to take the message of salvation to this world full of sin and pain."

Note: Paul Young passed away February 25, 1983.

Evelyn's Rhubarb Custard Pie

Make the pastry for a two-crust pie:
Mix:
   2 cups flour
   1 tsp. salt
   Cut in with pastry blender:
   2/3 c. lard

Add:
   1/4 c. cold water

Mix with fork or pastry blender until all the flour is moistened. Divide into two portions. Roll out on floured surface into a circle a little larger than the pie pan. Line the pan. Make filling and pour into pastry-lined pan. Cover with pastry top and bake according to directions.

For filling, beat slightly:
   3 eggs

Add:
   3 T. milk
   Mix and stir in:
   1 1/2 c. sugar
   1/4 c. flour
   3/4 tsp. nutmeg

Mix in:
   4 c. cut-up pink rhubarb

Pour into pastry-lined pan. Dot with butter. Cover with pastry top. Seal with fork or crimp with fingers. Make slits in top to let out steam. Sprinkle lightly with sugar. Bake until nicely browned. Serve slightly warm.

Temperature: 400 degrees.
Time: 45 to 50 minutes

A Heart for Imbabura is the sixth book in a continuing collection of missionary biographies. For more information on ordering other titles in the *Jaffray Collection of Missionary Portraits* contact your local Christian bookstore, or call Christian Publications toll-free **1-800-233-4443.** Ask to be put on the *Jaffray Collection of Missionary Portraits* mailing list. Then you will receive information when new titles are available.

Titles available as of Spring 1992:

Let My People Go
A.W. Tozer

"Weak Thing" in Moni Land
William Cutts

On Call
David Thompson

To China and Back
Anthony Bollback

Please Leave Your Shoes at the Door
Corrine Sahlberg

A Heart for Imbabura
Charles Shepson